INSIGHT

Capturing the Thoughts of God

JOE WILKES

Unveiling the Truth of God's Word
Inner Sight

Insight allows you to see deeper into the wisdom of God's Word and His ways. Insight is the pathway to the deeper things of God, which are only revealed by the Spirit of God. It takes you beyond what others see from the surface dimension. Insight causes your spiritual vision to be expanded.

> **1 Cor. 2: 9 & 10** *But as it is written, eye has not seen, nor ear heard, neither have it entered into the heart of man, the things which God hath prepared for them that love him. But God hath revealed them unto us by his Spirit: for the Spirit searcheth all things, yea, the deep things of God.*

Contents

Insight
Capturing the Thoughts of God

How and who inspired me to write this book?

It has become a way of life for me to set aside time for God. My wife and I, along with her sister and a very close friend, were vacationing in Orlando, Florida. My plan was to complete what I thought would be a workbook. My wife mentioned to this family friend (Ronda) that I was writing a book. With excitement in her voice, she said to me, "Pastor Joe, I heard you are writing a book. What's the title? How many words do have? What's the tagline? When are you planning on finishing? You know after you finish writing the first book, the publisher will be after you to write a second!"

Instantly, I was bombarded with a barrage of questions for which I had no answer. After all, in my mind, I was only supposed to be completing a workbook, one I had started five years ago. In a matter of minutes, I went from writing a workbook to writing a book with a second one to follow. My thoughts were, *God, we're moving kind of fast*. However, I understood her excitement, for she had recently written her first book. In doing so, she had volumes of wisdom and information to pass on to me. I didn't resist the thought of writing a book; instead, I embraced it.

For years, I have been writing thoughts on little sticky note pads. I have these notes in my vehicle, in my bibles, and on a cork board in my prayer room. They're everywhere. I have also recorded audio notes on a mini recorder that I keep with me at all times. I have come to understand I have been capturing the thoughts of God for years. Even as I am reading the scriptures, the Spirit of God illuminates specific words and verses, giving me insight. This is another way of saying He gives me "inside information."

The Contents of this Book

In this book, I share some of my personal experiences in capturing God's thoughts as He shared His insights with me. God wants to reveal His thoughts to His people.

The spiritual events that have taken place in my life may be hard for some to grasp. Therefore, I have provided several scriptures with each experience. I assure you, I am not trying to make the Word of God line up to support my spiritual experiences. However, my experiences must line up with the Word of God. It is very important to me that the information released via this book in no way contradicts what is written in the bible. This book reveals, explains, and clarifies several scriptures that the church seems to be in conflict over. The information in the latter portion of the book is filled with revelations that will help you understand the spiritual. My prayer is that you set aside your preconceived ideas and some of your past teachings and allow the Spirit of God to reveal to you the truth of His Word. If you do this, I believe you too will receive insight.

Over my past 35 years as a believer, I've listened to preachers and teachers from various denominations. When they explain some spiritual concepts, many leave me with questions they cannot answer. The Apostle Paul said, "I will not have you ignorant concerning the spiritual or spiritual things" (**1 Corinthians 12:1**) I do not have a monopoly on revelations into spiritual or spiritual things. However, I only ask that you read this book in its entirety. Also study the chapter on **Insight into the Spiritual** in the latter portion of this book. I, along with the disciples of Jesus, do not claim to be a bible scholar. The disciples were considered unlearned and ignorant by the religious leaders of their day. However, their minds were changed as they listened to the disciples speak. The scholars concluded the disciples must have been with Jesus.

The Apostle Paul was considered very educated but said he considered his prior religious status as nothing. He counted it as loss compared to the excellency of the knowledge of Christ. Paul also said the Word he was preaching and teaching did not come from man, but through revelation, the revealed knowledge or captured thoughts which gave him insight.

Chapter 1

Why Is Insight so Important?

In this book, we will be addressing two areas of insight that are important to every believer. The first area of insight is capturing the thoughts of God concerning people, places, and things. The second area of insight is the unveiling of what God is saying through His Word.

So many believers read the Word of God. So many hear the Word of God. So many teach the Word of God without insight. We send our children to so-called Christian schools, colleges, and universities. Why? To learn from people who we deem to be the best biblical teachers and scholars of our time. It seems to be a requirement, if we have any aspirations or desire to be in ministry. There is nothing wrong with getting a higher education in biblical learning. However, you can only learn up to the level of those who are teaching you. Over the past thirty-five years, I have read books and sat under the ministries of many men and women who were considered great and anointed teachers. As a young believer, it seemed as if there was so much to learn. I availed myself as much as I could. Later in life, I realized I had ingested some teachings that were not completely true. As a believer, something inside me desired the truth, the whole truth, and nothing but the truth. I understood that one half of the truth is as good as a lie. The truth gives birth to freedom, but the lie keeps you in bondage. I read in the bible where Jesus said this in **John 8:32** *"…and ye shall know the truth and the truth shall make you free."*

The word *know* means to be intimate with, as a man is intimate with his wife. This level of intimacy allows the woman to be impregnated by her husband. So, let's read this verse like this: "*…and ye shall be intimate with the truth and the truth that you are intimate with will impregnate you and cause you to give birth to freedom.*" As I said earlier, so many people are reading and hearing what God said, but not knowing nor understanding what it is that God is saying.

Insight moves you from not just hearing what God said, but understanding what He was saying, when He said what He said!

Without insight the enemy can and will twist the Word of God towards his advantage. We see this in Eve's encounter with the serpent in the garden of Eden.

Genesis 3:4, 5 *And the serpent said, unto the woman, ye shall not surely die: (5) For God doth know that in the day ye eat thereof, then your eyes shall be opened, and ye shall be as gods, knowing good and evil.*

Satan's methodology is to twist the Word so it is either deflated or inflated. It can be deflated to the point that it has lost its ability to reach or impact its designed target. Conversely, it could be inflated to the point where it overreaches its assigned target.

He tried to use that tactic on Jesus when he was in the wilderness (a place where there seems to be no provision).

Matthew 4:5-7 *Then the devil taketh him up into the holy city, and setteth him on a pinnacle of the temple. (6) And saith unto him, if thou be the Son of God, cast thyself down: for it is written, He will give his angels charge concerning thee: and in their hands they shall bear thee up, lest any time thou dash thy foot against a stone. (7) Jesus said unto him, It is written again, Thou shall not tempt the Lord thy God.*

If he tried this with Jesus, the living Word, do not think that you are somehow exempt!

Insight also moves you from not just knowing God's Word, but to knowing the truth of God's Word.

Apostle Paul, in his second letter to Timothy, said of some Christians, they were *"Ever learning, and never able to come to the knowledge of the truth."* **(2 Timothy 3:7)**

Jesus spoke with some in parables (Mark 4:10, 11). Some were satisfied with just hearing the parables. (They heard what He said.)

Others heard the same parable, yet they were not satisfied. They pursued Jesus and said, "Explain this parable to us."

Jesus referred to that parable as being a kingdom mystery. In other words, the meaning was unknown to man, yet given for some to not just hear, but to know the mysteries of the kingdom. I believe God gives insight to those who seek and desire to know the truth of His Word. I often wonder what would have happened if the apostles hadn't pursued Jesus for more understanding of that parable. I don't know if He would have given it to them.

In this dispensation, the Holy Spirit gives us insight into the mind of God. Listen to what Jesus said in these passages of scripture:

John 16:12-13, 15b *I have yet many things to say unto you, but ye cannot bear them now. (13) Howbeit, when he, the Spirit of truth, is come, he will guide you into all truth: for he shall not speak of himself; but whatsoever he shall hear, that shall he speak: and he will shew you things to come. (15b) therefore said I, that he shall take of mine, and shall shew it unto you.*

Not some truth, not half of the truth, not just one area of truth, nor one subject of truth. The Holy Spirit will show you the truth, but He is not going to force the truth on you. If you are satisfied with a lack of the truth, it's on you and not on God. He said, *"My people are destroyed* (perishing) *for lack of knowledge: because thou hast rejected knowledge, I will also reject thee."* **(Hosea 4:6)**

If you desire truth, God said, the Holy Spirit will guide and lead you to all truth, but you must follow Him.

As I mentioned earlier, I have learned things from many fine anointed men and women of God. However, they could not impart insight to me. I have found the best teacher. He sits in the highest office of learning. He is the CEO of Kingdom University, and He has taught me much and given me insight. The Spirit of the living God is the best teacher from whom we can ever learn. His school of learning is open 24 hours a day and 7 days a week. He never sleeps nor slumbers and reveals nothing but truth.

> **1 John 2:26, 27** *These things have I written unto concerning them that seduce you. (27) But the anointing which ye have received of him abideth in you, and ye need not that any man teach you: but as the same anointing teacheth you of all things, and is truth, and is no lie, and even as it has taught you, ye shall abide in him.*

There are so many things the Spirit of God has shown me about insight. I will share more in later chapters of this book.

As for now, let's dive into the main topic of the book, which dovetails into the subject of insight.

Chapter 2

What the Holy Spirit Showed Me about Capturing the Thoughts of God

Maintaining Captured Thoughts

The thoughts of God must not only be captured, but also maintained.

The Lord showed me a vision of a person standing inside a glass tube. This tube looked like what they use in some gameshow challenges where money is flying around in the air and the person inside the tube tries to grab as much money as possible. What was so different about the game I saw in the vision was that some of the dollars flying around in the glass tube were counterfeit. Another challenge was that the person must have the ability to hold onto the real money they captured while trying to acquire more. My interpretation of this vision was this: There are many thoughts in the atmosphere. Not every thought comes from God. Some thoughts may have the appearance of legitimacy or being from God, but they are not. Even after you capture the thoughts of God, you must also maintain them.

There have been times when the Holy Spirit gave me a thought. I said to myself, *That's good. I'm going to remember that.* Five minutes later, it was gone. I had captured the thought of God but did not maintain it. I was distracted by something that took my spiritual mind and focus away from what I knew was the thought of God. Sometimes the enemy will use another thought to distract you while you are in the process of capturing the thoughts of God.

Mark 4:15 *And these are they by the way side where the word is sown; but when they have heard,* **Satan cometh immediately**, *and taketh away the word that was sown in their hearts.* (Emphasis mine.)

Where Did that Thought Come From?

As we capture thoughts, we must ask ourselves: Where did that thought come from? Many of God's people have made wrong decisions, wrong turns, and wrong statements because they captured, meditated, and acted on the wrong thoughts. Many have doubted their purpose and even questioned their call because they captured thoughts that originated from the kingdom of darkness. Some who were settled and stable suddenly became unsettled and unstable as they entertained the wrong thoughts. I call these thoughts, the "AM I?" thoughts. They generate questions such as, "Am I really called to do this or that? Am I really called to be here or there?"

When you capture the thoughts of God, they don't open the door to questions of doubt, unbelief, or fear. They leave you with thoughts of assuredness and certainty. Remember, God did not reveal himself in the form of a question when Moses asked His identity.

Exodus 3:13 *And Moses said unto God, Behold, when I come unto the children of Israel, and shall say unto them, The God of your fathers hath sent me unto you; and they say what is his name? what shall I say unto them? (14) And God said unto Moses, I AM THAT I AM: and he said, Thus shalt thou say unto the children of Israel, I AM hath sent me unto you.*

God did not reveal himself in the form of a question, but as the firm, solid, and confident answer (I AM), not "Am I?" Glory to God!

Chapter 3

Capturing of Thoughts

Three Origins of Thoughts

It is extremely important to understand that we are in a constant mode of capturing thoughts. The thoughts that we capture have a direct effect on our actions. Thoughts proceed and give birth to actions and speech. There are *three origins* of thoughts that Jesus identified in addressing Peter's actions and speech. In **Matthew 16**, Jesus spoke to his disciples concerning his death, burial, and resurrection. In verse 22, "*Then Peter took him, and began to rebuke him, saying, Be it far from thee, Lord: this shall not be unto thee. (23) But he* (Jesus) *turned and said unto Peter, Get thee behind me, Satan: thou art an offence* (stumbling block) *unto me: for thou savourest* (feel or think) *not the things that be of God, but those that be of men.*"

Jesus mentions the names *Satan, Man,* and *God* in addressing Peter's thoughts and feelings. From this scripture, it is safe to say there are three origins of thoughts. The thoughts of man, the thoughts of Satan, and the thoughts of God.

The Thoughts of Man

The thoughts of man often originate from our five physical senses (sight, touch, taste, smell, and hearing). What you hear with your natural ears, see with your natural eyes, touch with your natural hands, taste with your natural tongue, and smell with your natural nose can all induce thought patterns. Your thoughts originate from the natural arena in which you live. Your thoughts may often focus on how something can benefit you. They may seem to be good ideas, but they are not God ideas.

Note: Thoughts, words, and actions can impact the earth realm. Thoughts that originate from man in the earth realm, released in the form of words or actions, can impact both the natural and spiritual realm.

The Thoughts of Satan

The thoughts of Satan and the thoughts of God both come from the realm of the spirit. The thoughts that exist in the spirit realm are designed for man to receive and release via words or actions. Notice what Jesus said to Peter, "Get thee behind me, Satan." Jesus knew the source of that thought and immediately addressed the words Peter spoke. Although the words appeared to be harmless, they did not advance God's kingdom. Therefore, Jesus deemed them satanic in origin.

It says in **John 13:2**, "*...the devil having now put into the heart of Judas Iscariot, Simon's son, to betray him (Jesus)...*"

Before those words entered Judas's heart, they first entered his head via his thoughts. Then from his heart, the words proceeded into actions.

Peter, in dealing with Ananias in **Acts 5:3**, said, "*...why hath Satan filled thine heart to lie to the Holy Ghost, and to keep back part of the price of the land?*" Again, here is an example of wrong thoughts, wrong words, and wrong actions. Jesus, as He walked on the earth as a man, made this statement in **John 6:63b**, "*...the words that I speak unto you, they are spirit, and they are life.*"

The messenger angel who was sent to Daniel stated this:

Daniel 10:11-13: "*...O Daniel, a man greatly beloved, understand the words that I speak unto thee, and stand upright: for* *unto thee I am now sent. And when he had spoken this word unto me, I stood trembling. (12) Then said he unto me, Fear not, Daniel: for from the first day that thou didst set thine heart to understand, and to chasten thyself before thy God, **thy words were heard**, and **I am come for thy words**. (13) But **the prince of the kingdom of Persia withstood me** one and twenty days: but, lo, Michael, one of the chief princes, came to help me; and I remained there with the kings of Persia."* (Emphasis mine.)

As you can see from this passage, a direct thought and action from a man in the earth realm praying for twenty-one days had an impact on the spiritual realm. Words released in the natural realm were heard, which caused actions (movement) in the spiritual realm. Listen again to what the angel said, "…thy words were heard, and I am come for (as a result of) thy words."

Daniel's thoughts, released in the form of words, were heard in the realm of the spirit by both the angel of God and the forces of darkness. The messenger angel was coming with the answer and the Prince of Persia came to withstand (hinder) him. This resulted in twenty-one days of warfare in the spirit realm. This warfare in the spirit started because of the words released by Daniel's prayer in the natural realm.

Be mindful of this important fact before you put your thoughts into words: Something will happen because of what you release from your mouth in the form of words.

Chapter 4

Holding Thoughts Captive

(Confrontation in the Mind)

Some thoughts must be immediately interrupted!

Wrong thoughts in your mind can impact your actions and emotions.

Have you ever had an argument or confrontation with someone in your mind? In your mind, in your thinking, you are conversing with someone who is not present. You are saying things to them, and they are answering you, in your mind. This mental conversation turns into an argument. Isn't it amazing that in these mental conversations the other person or persons' response never seems to be one of compliance, but to the contrary, one of combat? You find yourself getting angry, and your countenance begins to change. In some cases, you may notice your fist beginning to clench. You are being impacted by wrong thoughts that you have captured and brought into your thought process. Before you realize it, you meditate about this for hours, thinking about how these thoughts have impacted your actions. You can be assured that these thoughts did not come from God.

This is a setup by the enemy before you encounter the person with whom you have been engaged in thought warfare. That thought process must be immediately interrupted and resolved.

The Capture and Release Mode

When the enemy sneaks a thought in, and I recognize it, I have learned to implement a Capture and Release procedure. I hold that thought captive, (it has now been interrupted). In other words, it can't go any further. I am now ready to release that thought. I say audibly and emphatically, "**That's not my thought!**" When the thought tries to linger, I may say this several times until it has released from my mind.

Note: If you don't hold the enemy's thoughts captive, they will capture you. I release them from my mind by saying, "That's not my thought." Then I close the door by releasing what God's Word says about that thought or situation.

Releasing Others from Your Wrong Thoughts
(The Bitter Root)

The Word of God tells us not to be ignorant of the devil's devices or strategies. As a pastor, I've seen the enemy's strategies at work through God's people when they capture the wrong thoughts. I've seen where one member of the church or body of Christ has a conflict with another member and they become hurt and embittered. A thought comes to them saying, "You need to share what was done or said about you by Sister So-and-So." The enemy of the church is not satisfied with you sharing your situation or imaginations with just one person. He wants these wrong thoughts to impact everyone around you. Soon, other people are infected and become angry with that person. You have defiled other people with what troubled you.

> **Hebrews 12:15** *Looking diligently lest any man fail the grace of God; lest any root of bitterness **springing up trouble you, and many be defiled**... (Emphasis mine.)

Listen to what is being conveyed in this passage of scripture. Let's apply it to the above example. Be aware, alert, and on guard lest any man fail (come behind, be found lacking) in their ability to extend God's grace to others. If you fail to operate in the grace of God, it can result in a root of bitterness, something deeply embedded in your thoughts, that is released in the form of words and actions. The passage states, **springing up trouble you.** You find yourself thinking about it every day. The moment you wake in the morning, the enemy feeds those thoughts to you and you embrace them. You are now captured by the wrong thoughts. It's not enough for *you* to be troubled. The enemy wants that wrong thought to defile (make unclean) others too. **You are troubled and you have defiled others.**

Now time has passed, and you have allowed God to heal you of all the hurts and pains of that past situation. You are now cleansed, and you no longer have any bad or ill thoughts or feelings towards that person. God has done such a work within you, that you have now become close with the person for whom you once had ill feelings and wrong thoughts. Everything seems to be okay, and you capture a thought of God, which says, **"You must release others from your wrong thoughts!"** Remember, what was said in Hebrews, **you were troubled and caused others to be defiled.**

One might ask, "How do I release others from my past wrong thoughts?" It's simple, go to them and repent. Let them know you have been healed and you were wrong in how you handled things. Ask them to forgive you and pray with them.

When you pray, command that every negative word that was released out of your mouth, that produced wrong thoughts in others, be bound in Jesus' name. Declare that the powers of darkness have no more authority to use those thoughts or words to defile and divide. Ask God to release you and others from the bondage of those words. *(In Jesus' name.)*

> **Matthew 16:19** *And I will give unto thee the keys of the kingdom of heaven: and whatsoever thou shalt bind on earth shall be bound in heaven: and whatsoever thou shalt loose on earth shall be loosed in heaven.*

Bringing Thoughts into the Obedience of God

Thoughts must be held captive so we can bring them into the obedience of God's Word. Let's examine what the Holy Spirit said via the Apostle Paul's letter to the church:

> **2 Corinthians 10:4, 5** *(For the weapons of our warfare are not carnal, but mighty through God to pulling down of strong holds;) (5) Casting down imaginations, and every high thing that exalteth itself against the knowledge of God, and bringing into captivity every thought to the obedience of Christ…*

Key words:

1. **Strongholds** (fortress, to fortify for the purpose of safely holding): they must be pulled down! Anything the enemy can use to fortify his position in your thought process.
2. **Imaginations** (thoughts that can be visual): they must be cast down! It started out as an imagination and evolved into a stronghold because it was not dealt with (cast down).
3. **High Thing** (lofty arguments or high opinions of oneself): Imagination joins forces with high things to exalt itself (to lift up, to be in a high position) in your mind.
4. **Against:** to oppose, to be at war with the knowledge of God.
5. **Knowledge:** God's knowledge or thoughts about people, places, or things.

Because thoughts give birth to actions, God says, "*Every* thought must be brought into captivity." These captured thoughts must be scrutinized, interrogated, and separated. They must pass the obedience test and meet certain criteria before they are fit for your thinking. They must be properly vetted before they are released as words or actions in the earth realm.

There are also thoughts and words that exist in the spirit realm that God wants released in the earth realm. The same could be said about Satan.

What the Word Says about Separating

Matthew13:47, 48 *Again the Kingdom of heaven is like unto a net, that was cast into the sea, and gathered of every kind: (48) Which, when it was full, they drew to shore, and sat down, and gathered the good into vessels, but **cast the bad away**.* (Emphasis mine.)

Matthew 25:31, 32 *When the Son of man shall come in his glory, and all the holy angels with him, then shall he sit upon the throne of his glory: (32) And before him shall be gathered all nations: and he shall **separate them** one from another, as a shepherd **divideth** his sheep from the goats… (Emphasis mine.)*

2 Timothy 2:15 *Study to shew thyself approved unto God, a workman that needed not be ashamed, **rightly dividing** the word of truth. (Emphasis mine.)*

As you can see from these scriptures, God has no problem with separating and dividing. As believers, it is very important that we properly vet every thought that tries to access our minds. If we allow wrong words to enter, they will impact the words we release from our mouths and the actions that may follow.

Chapter 5

Capturing the Thoughts of God

Capturing Pictorial Thoughts

The Holy Spirit showed me other things about capturing the thoughts of God. Sometimes God's thoughts come in pictorial form. These pictures can flash before you like a movie playing at rapid speed, one frame at a time. As you seize, capture, and lay hold of that one picture, you realize it is a thought of God. You must understand that the pictorial thought is not the whole thing. It is just a sample of something much bigger.

Here is an example: Have you ever been in a Sam's Club where they are handing out little food samples? When you try one, you have just captured a sample. The next thing you know, you are asking, "Where can I get the whole bag?"

Here's another example: You are sitting in a meeting, and someone says, "I have a thought. What if…?" They reveal their thought about the subject matter that's being discussed. From that one thought, the group begins to pursue it, build on it, and add to it. Before long, that thought has blossomed into something much larger.

That's how it is when you capture the thoughts of God. That one thought causes you to seek God for the entirety of His thoughts on that subject. Capturing the thought of God causes you to desire the rest of the story.

Once a thought is captured, the next step is to build around it. As you begin to pray and seek the Lord, He begins to release more into your spiritual mind. As you study his Word, clarity comes and protects you from the enemy's ability to sow weeds into the harvesting of thoughts.

Sometimes God will give multiple messages in one thought! Be mindful that the thought is just a thought. You must seek God for the details!

Chapter 6

Thoughts and Ways

(Thoughts Can Direct a Person's Ways)

Proverbs 14:12 *There is a way which seemeth right unto a man, but the end thereof are the ways of death.*

As natural men and women, we often believe the way we are doing things or the path we have chosen is right. In life, we have so many decisions to make. According to our thoughts and rationale, we may think we are making the right decisions. In times of uncertainty, we consult others, and they may agree we have made the right decision. However, according to this passage in Proverbs, "There is a way which seemeth right unto a man." Notice it did not say it was right unto God!

The way that seems right to man, when taken to its logical conclusion, results in death and destruction.

Imagine spending so much time believing a certain thing or doing certain things a certain way, to finally arrive at the end of it, and realize God was not in it.

Because our thoughts often govern our ways, it is very important that we capture and hold onto God's thoughts and not man's.

We need to know what God's thoughts are concerning people, places, and things, and not man's thoughts or traditions.

Isaiah 55:8 *For my thoughts are not your thoughts, neither are your ways my ways, saith the Lord.*

As we can see from this verse, there is a conflict between God's thoughts and man's thoughts. God separates Himself from man's thoughts by saying, *"They are not my thoughts!"*

Not only does He separate himself from man's thoughts, but He also rejects man's ways by saying, "Your ways are not my ways!"

God knows that thoughts and ways (actions) go hand in hand, so He addresses them both together, yet separately.

Even in verse 7 He calls for the wicked to forsake their ways and the unrighteous to forsake their thoughts. Before we can embrace God's thoughts and ways, we must first forsake (give up, leave, abandon) our own.

What is the benefit of forsaking our thoughts and ways?

We will never be able to capture God's thoughts which lead to His ways if we are not willing to forsake our own.

Higher Thoughts

Isaiah 55:9 *For as the heavens are higher than the earth, so are my ways higher than your ways and my thoughts than your thoughts.*

If you'll notice, the Lord made a comparison where heaven represents his thoughts, and the earth represents our thoughts. This comparison depicts how much higher heaven is from the earth.

Even in the natural world, we exert a tremendous amount of energy and money in our efforts to go higher. When satellites were sent up into space (higher place), it caused a rapid shift in the technology industry. This gave many countries access to all sorts of information and warfare advantages. So many things happened because man had the willingness to going higher.

As believers, we must desire to go higher. It is imperative that we capture God's thoughts. In these days of extreme warfare, God wants the church to be ready to capture His thoughts and ways to gain spiritual advantage over our enemy.

A Captured Thought of God

One morning after reading a chapter from the book *God's Generals*, my thoughts immediately shifted to our young people. I was thinking about how so many of them don't have a true relationship with God, even though they attend church on Sundays and Wednesdays. I could hear their angry voices. They were angry because they were being raised in homes abandoned by their earthly fathers. Some were living in lack and poverty, not of their own making, but because they lived in a single-parent home. Something inside them was questioning if God was really real and if so, why were they living like this?

I could hear the voices of wives who had lost their beloved husbands and mothers who had lost their sons to street violence. I could hear the words of others echoing within me, "Why, God? Why do You allow this to happen to me?" Blaming God for all the misfortunes, abuses, and catastrophes seemed to be the norm. Then, I heard these words from deep within my spirit, "Your beef (issue, problem) is not with Me, but with the devil!" So many people young and old blame God, which is the plan of the enemy, diverting the focus off himself. Look at what God says and what His answer is to all of life's woes:

John 10:10 *The thief cometh no, but for to steal, kill, and to destroy: I am come that they might have life, and that they might have it more abundantly.*

Acts 10:38 *How God anointed Jesus of Nazareth with the Holy Ghost and with power: who went about doing good, and healing all that were oppressed of the devil; for God was with him.*

3 John 1:2 *Beloved, I wish above all things that thou mayeth prosper and be in health, even as thy soul prospereth.*

God's people have been barking up the wrong tree, in God's face blaming Him for the things the devil has done to them. After doing so, the devil points at God, telling people that God took your son, your daughter, or your husband. From what I see in the bible, everyone who God took was alive.

Enoch walked with God and was no more.

Elijah was taken up in a whirlwind.

Jesus was taken by God in a cloud.

Get out of the face of God and get on your face before God!

As the church learns to capture God's thoughts, these thoughts will put us in the position of winning and never settling for defeat.

Chapter 7

Capturing God's Thoughts
Via Dreams and Visions

Sometimes God will speak to his people via dreams and visions. This is another way to capture the thoughts of God. In Acts 10, Peter had a vision where he captured the thoughts of God concerning salvation coming to the gentiles. The vision God gave to Peter is considered an open vision, when a person is awake, and their eyes are open. God allows them to see pictures in a movie format. It seems like they're watching a movie play out right before their eyes. In those cases, God may be trying to reveal something that advances His kingdom agenda. In the vision Peter had, God also gave him verbal instructions as to what he was to do.

God Gave Me a Vision

Years ago, as a young believer, I was attending a church where my spiritual growth had come to a standstill. I knew there was more to God than what I was experiencing. The Word I was hearing no longer challenged me. Although I had reached a spiritual plateau, my love for my church family caused me to be complacent. My hunger for more of God led me to visit other churches on Sunday nights.

Finally, I came to accept that God was leading me out of the church which had been very instrumental in my initial spiritual growth. I knew God was calling me out, but I wasn't sure where he wanted me to go. I was also concerned I would miss the will of God.

I said, "Lord, I'm not leaving this church until I know that I know you are leading me." Every day I would go into the spare bathroom and seek God.

One day as I went into that room to pray, with the lights off and my eyes closed, God gave me a vison. In the vision, he showed me a graduation ceremony, where I along with others were dressed in caps and gowns. We were graduating from what seemed to be the 2nd grade. I had just captured a thought of God via a closed vision. A **closed vision** is somewhat like an **open vision**, except one takes place while your eyes are open, and the other takes place while your eyes are closed. However, in both cases, you are awake. Even though I saw that vision, I was still very cautious, and I asked the Lord to give me another sign.

God Gave Me A Dream

As I had been praying, I said, "Lord, I'll do what You want me to do. I just need to know it's You who is leading me." Not long after that, God gave me a dream. In the scriptures, God often spoke to people through dreams, sometimes referred to as visions in the night.

> **Job 33:14-17** *For God speaketh once, yea twice, yet man perceiveth it not. (15) In a dream, in a vision of the night, when deep sleep falleth upon men, in slumbering upon the bed; (16) Then he openeth the ears of men, and sealeth their instruction, (17) That he may withdraw man from his purpose and hide pride from man.*

The dream God gave me took place in the church I was attending. In the dream, I was having a conversation with a person in the church for whom I had a lot of respect. I was telling that individual that I felt God was calling me out of that church. Immediately, that individual began to rebuke me and told me I was missing God as they walked away. I started to be overwhelmed with confusion, because in the dream it appeared that I valued the opinion of that person in whom I was confiding. With tears in my eyes, I sat on the front pew, then another person walked by and spoke these words to me:

"You better obey God!"

I woke up with that dream permanently branded in my mind. In the dream, God did not show me the faces of those two people. I had no idea who they were. I didn't even know whether they were male or female. However, in the dream I know the first person was somewhat tall and the second person was short.

The Unveiling of the Dream

As the weeks went on after the dream, it seemed as if it was just a dream that had no significance. Then it happened after a Sunday morning service. I was standing in the church next to the front pew. I was having a conversation with my Sunday school teacher who was a somewhat tall lady for whom I had great respect. I told her, "I believe the Lord is leading me out of this church."

She immediately rebuked me as she replied, "You're missing God!"

I sat down on the front pew, confused and wondering if I was indeed missing God and what should I do? Then Brother Willie, who happened to be short in stature, walked by me and said, **"You better obey God!"**

I sat there with tears in my eyes, then God reminded me of the dream He had given me. I left church that day with peace in my heart, knowing God was directing me. I had to obey Him, for He was leading me out of one place into another place of destiny. Little did I know at that time, I had captured the thoughts of God via a dream.

I believe that God has been speaking to His people in various ways, yet we have not perceived that it was Him who was speaking. My prayer is that our hearts and minds will now be open to capture the thoughts of God.

Chapter 8

A Preseason Captured Thought

I've heard it said that God will show up or give you what you need in due season. The Apostle Paul wrote to the church in Galatia that they would reap in **due** (one's own) **season** (a fixed or definite time). It has also been said that God is always on time. I have also come to realize that God will have you capture thoughts in your preseason. What do I mean by preseason? It's a word given in advance to deal with something that has yet to show up on your radar, a thought captured that you are not aware as to how or where to apply it at that time. However, that captured word is very important, although it may not yet seem to be. The word that He gives you in your preseason is to be valued, held onto, and carried over into your due season. It will sustain you and bring you victory in due time.

*God will speak a word to you in your **preseason** that you must capture, hold onto, and carry into your **due season**. I captured a thought of God, a word given to me. This was a short word that burned in my spirit to the point that I had to put it on my recorder. Little did I know that the words captured would become so vital to my victory in the battle that I faced with Covid-19 in December of 2020.*

These are the words that God spoke which I captured as a thought:

Don't allow your feelings to be the guardian of your faith!

At 3:38 pm on July 31, 2019, the Lord spoke this very important word to me. God will speak a word to you, not only in your due season, but also in your preseason.

He said, "Joe, your feelings can never be the guardian of your faith."

Little did I realize how important that revelation would be to me. Over the years through life's experiences, I've learned that feelings are attached to the sense arena and will always check in with my flesh before delivering its report.

Feelings or any of the other senses are incapable of guarding your faith. To walk by faith, you must leave the senses arena and your focus must be on what the Word of God says concerning any and everything you may be facing. Come hell or high water, God's Word must be the final authority. Too often we look at other people's outcome to determine the validity of God's word. Some may say, "Well, sister, brother, or Pastor So-and-So, they were good Christians and look what happened to them." However, the Word of God tells us in **Hebrews 12:2** *"Looking unto Jesus the author and finisher of our faith..."* The only thing that has the capacity to guard the God kind of faith is the God kind of Word!

> **Romans 10:17** *So then faith cometh by hearing, and hearing by the word of God.*

This was when my physical body came under attack by the Covid-19 virus. Doctors were saying there was nothing they could do, and there was no so-called vaccine at that time. I did the things I needed to do in the natural. I stayed hydrated, took vitamins, and got plenty of rest. I was also battling this invisible enemy with the Word of God. I found myself becoming agitated with those around me, those who loved me and were concerned about me. They would ask, "How are you feeling?"

My response was, "Please don't ask me that again!"

When my son asked, "Dad, how are you feeling?"

I said to him, "Don't ask me that, but tell me what the Word of God says about me."

He instantly replied, "You are healed."

My response was, "That's what I'm talking about. Now we have a connection."

During my battle, I came to understand that I could not leave the faith arena and check into the feeling arena to determine if God's Word was at work in my physical body. Remember what God spoke to me: "Your feeling can't ever be the guardian of your faith." However, your faith can always stand as the guardian for how you feel and how you view things. I am thankful to God for His preseason insight that ushered me into victory during my Covid-19 battle.

2 Corinthians 5:7 *For we walk by faith, not by sight…* (the sense arena).

Chapter 9

INSIGHT
Insight by Way of Experience

Some may say that experience is the *best* teacher, but I have come to learn that experience can be a *powerful* teacher. One night, my family and I along with some other friends attended a ministers' conference in Tulsa, Oklahoma. Prior to this meeting, I had been taught and believed that the Holy Spirit was a perfect gentleman. I was told he would not force you to do anything that you did not want to do. To set the stage for the upcoming event, we were seated in what I remember as the eighth row up on the side seats of this huge auditorium. It was a night when an offering would be collected for the school and all the students were attending this service. Something happened to me in that service that I will never forget, and I can't deny, even if the enemy tries to tell me I'm imagining it. God did this in front of hundreds of people, along with the ones who accompanied me to that service, and they will never let me forget it.

This transpired in 1996. The speaker took the stage, and with great expectation and anticipation, I was prepared to hear the Word of the Lord. As the singers on stage continued to sing praises to God, we were all standing on our feet, clapping our hands, and participating in praising the Lord. I could feel the change in the atmosphere and could see the Glory of God on the speaker, as he stood on the stage. After a while, he slowly began to come down from the platform and walked amongst the people. Although he was some distance away from me, I could hear a sound emanating from his lapel microphone. I could hear him saying, "Sha, Sha, Sha," as he walked up and down the aisles. Then he would stop and look at certain individuals and begin to laugh. As he laughed, there seemed to be an anointing that was released, and it came down on the people. When this hit certain individuals, the preacher would just stand there. I watched as some fell backwards, some fell to their knees, and some would even twirl like a spinning top. This manifestation began to spontaneously break out in the upper parts of the auditorium. As I watched, some began to run at an amazing speed under the anointing. Things happen under the anointing that are impossible under normal circumstances.

While under the anointing, Elijah outran a chariot.

1 Kings 18:46 *And the hand of the Lord was on Elijah; and he girded up his loins and* **ran** *before Ahab to the entrance of Jezreel.* (Emphasis mine.)

MY Last Laugh

As I watched things unfold, I became a spectator. The events were funny to me, and I began to laugh. I was not laughing in the glory; I was laughing at what people were doing under the anointing. I can remember a young lady who had a dress on that was narrow at the bottom trying to run as the glory fell on her. Because her dress was so narrow at the bottom, she could only take little bitty steps. Can you imagine trying to run at a rapid speed under the anointing with that type of limitation? After running about twenty feet, she fell on her belly and began to rock like a rocking chair. Although all these things were happening, no one was hurt, for it was a true move of the Spirit of God.

The preacher moved closer to where I was standing. I was praising God, clapping my hands, while still laughing at the previous event with the young lady. Suddenly, something hit me. It was like someone had grabbed me by the front of my shirt.

It was saying, "It's your turn now."

I can remember saying out loud, "I don't want to do this!"

The next thing I knew, I was snatched out into the aisle, and something hit me that I could not contain. It felt like I was on fire, and my actions were as if I was trying to put this fire out amid a whirlwind.

I know what it feels like to have your clothing catch fire and the action that accompanies it. When I was a young child, I was in the backyard *playing with fire*. My Davy Crockett pants, with little tassels on the outer edge, caught on fire. I tried my best to use my hands to put the fire out. Then I stopped, dropped to the ground, and began to roll around until the fire was extinguished.

The fire of God is different. It doesn't burn painfully but impacts you in a way that causes you to immediately respond to it. It's like an inward burning that requires an outward response.

Jeremiah said, "It was like fire shut up in my bones."

Immediately, I went from a standing position eight rows up, down to the floor level on my face. My suit jacket was halfway off, and my tie had wrapped around my neck and was slung over my back shoulder. I had no idea where my glasses were. I tried to rise to my feet, but my legs felt like wet spaghetti. Some of the ushers noticed me struggling to get up and came over to help me get seated in the nearest available ground-level seat. My feelings and actions were like a man who was intoxicated. As they lifted me up from the ground, I remember saying something to them that now seems so stupid.

I said, "I would have you know that I am a dignified man."

Instantly I had gone from being a spectator to becoming a participant, and now people were laughing at me. Because the service was being recorded and the video was broadcast to the entire auditorium, everyone could see what happened to me. My son was attending the youth service and had heard that people were laughing at some man who was overcome by the power of God. Unbeknownst to him, they were laughing at his dad.

My wife shared that when the Holy Spirit got ahold of me, my Pastor friend Carl, who was also standing and laughing with me, immediately sat down and grabbed the bottom of his chair and began to hold on as if he was strapping himself in.

So much for the myth that the Holy Spirit is a perfect gentleman and will not force you to do anything you don't want to do. My last words were, "I don't want to do this!" Without my consent, it happened to me anyway. What I experienced was a move of God that was like fire mixed with a whirlwind.

When that fire and wind hits, it moves things instantly. The writer of the Book of Acts, in trying to describe Pentecost, would use words *as of* and *like as of*. He mentioned it being as a rushing (moving), mighty (forceful) wind accompanied by fire.

> **Acts 2:2** *And suddenly there came a sound from heaven as of a **rushing mighty wind**, and it filled all the house where they were sitting.* (V3) *And there appeared unto them cloven tongues **like as of fire** and it sat upon each of them.* (Emphasis mine.)

Chapter 10

I Asked the Holy Spirit for Insight

O ne night while teaching bible study, we were reading a passage of scripture for which I thought I had a pretty good grasp. I had read these verses several times in my thirty-five years of being saved. I had listened to so many ministers give an interpretation of what these bible verses meant. Some I agreed with, and others I didn't. I taught these scriptures in line with those with which I agreed.

Scripture Insight

Romans 8:26, 27 *Likewise the Spirit also helpeth our infirmities: for we know not what we should pray for as we ought: but the Spirit itself maketh intercession for us with groanings which cannot be uttered. (27) And he that searcheth the hearts knoweth what is the mind of the Spirit, because he maketh intercession for the saints according to the will of God.*

For years I had been taught what these two verses were saying. What I heard and learned from ministers is what I preached. At that time, the interpretations I heard all seemed to be legitimate. Here are some of the things I heard about these two verses:

Sometimes we don't know how to pray as we should. The Holy Spirit helps us when we pray in tongues. We pray in words that are too deep to be understood or uttered in the words of man. (Note: This was the basis for praying in a language we and others did not understand.)

Another interpretation was: "This is when the Holy Spirit uses you to pray with moanings and groanings," also referred to as deep uncontrollable intercessions.

What I had been taught seemed to be that God would use man to pray with the help or aid of the Holy Spirit. It wasn't until one of my members said, "This is God the father using the Holy Spirit in intercessional prayers for us."

With that statement, I felt challenged to investigate this passage of scripture for myself. I quickly concluded that there was something missing. Something just wasn't adding up in what I had been taught and preached to all these years. The comment made during the Wednesday night bible study started me on a quest to find what was missing in my understanding of this passage. I began to pray and ask the Holy Spirit to reveal to me what we were missing in this passage of scripture, and He did.

As we begin to dissect these two scriptures, there is something important we must understand. In the eighth chapter of Romans, what is the main focus? We can clearly see through verses 1 through 25 that the Spirit is mentioned repeatedly. Walking after the Spirit; being led by the Spirit; being Spiritually minded; the Spirit of Christ in you; the works of the Spirit; the Spirit of him who raised Christ from the dead: the Spirit will quicken your mortal bodies; the Spirit beareth witness with our spirits; and the Spirit will mortify the deeds of the flesh:

> **Romans 8:26, 27** *Likewise the Spirit also helpeth our infirmities: for we know not what we should pray for as we ought: but the Spirit itself maketh intercession for us with groanings which cannot be uttered. (27) And he that searcheth the hearts knoweth what is the mind of the Spirit, because he maketh intercession for the saints according to the will of God.*

Let's dissect these two verses word by word. Let's start with the word *likewise*, which means, also or moreover. In the same way as the

Spirit helped or aided us in the previous verses, the Spirit helps or aids in our infirmities or weaknesses. In this passage, in what area are we weak? It says we need help in the area of prayer. What's wrong with our prayers? We don't know what we should pray for! In other words, we are praying in the wrong way, praying for the wrong things, praying in the wrong areas, and sometimes praying for the wrong people.

This scripture also has a rebuke to the Church when it comes to praying in the wrong way. It said, "We don't know what to pray for **as we ought**." It says we ought or should know what to pray for, but because we lack spiritual insight or do not seek God in prayer, we pray in the wrong way. Therefore, the Spirit Himself must help us. How? Through intercessions (stand in the gap, step in, intercede) for us. Notice it said, *for us* and not *through us* as some would have us believe. What kind of intercessions is the Spirit making? The scripture says it is with groanings (to sigh, a long, deep audible breath) that cannot be uttered or expressed in words. We can see from this scripture that the Spirit is not praying for us, he is interceding for us. How does that work? This is where verse 27 comes in and gives more understanding.

> **Verse 27** *And he that searcheth the hearts knoweth what is the mind of the Spirit, because he maketh intercession for the saints according to the will of God.*

In this verse, there is a person identified as *he* that we must identify. Who is this *he* that is making intercession for the saints? Some have thought this was the Holy Spirit, because in verse 27 it says that he "maketh intercession for us." Some have also said, this *he* that is mentioned in this verse is God the Father. I tend to differ with both of those assumptions, and this is why. This *he* cannot be referring to God the Father. This verse says *he* "maketh intercession for the saints according to the will of God." This could not be God the Father making intercession (standing in the gap) for us *to himself* according to His will.

Let's deal with why this verse cannot be referring to the Holy Spirit of God. First it says that this *he* "searcheth the heart and knoweth the mind of the Spirit." This *he* is not the Spirit searching the heart and knowing the mind (thoughts and purposes) *of himself*. Secondly, we read in the previous verse that the Spirit made intercessions with groanings, not words. This person is making intercession according to the will of God and we know God's will is His Word. This person is interceding with the Word of God.

Now that we know who this *he* is not, let's find out from the scripture who this *he* is. The answer is found in verse 34, right under our noses, and we've overlooked it all these years.

Romans 8:34 *Who is he that condemneth?* **It is Christ** *that died, yea rather, that is risen again, who is even at the right hand of God,* **who ever maketh intercession** *for us.* (Emphasis mine.)

Hebrews 7:24, 25 *But this man (Jesus) because he continueth ever, has an unchangeable priesthood. (25) Wherefore he is able also to save them to the uttermost that come unto God by him, seeing* **he ever liveth to make intercession** *for them. (Emphasis mine.)*

I conclude, the *he* that Romans 8:27 is referring to is no other than Jesus Christ Himself. He is also known as the Word of God!

John 1:1, 2 says, *"In the beginning was the Word, and the Word was with God, and the Word was God. (2) The same was in the beginning with God."*

Revelations 19:13 *And he was clothed with a vesture dipped in blood: and his name is called The Word of God.*

This is the reality of Romans 8:26 and 27, and this is how it works:
1. When we are praying the wrong way, this causes the Spirit to intercede (step in).

2. The Holy Spirit begins to groan (sigh) in grief at us for not praying correctly.
3. Jesus, the One who searches the heart, knows the mind (thoughts and purpose) of the Spirit and hears Him groan. They are so close that He knows why the Spirit is groaning.
4. When Jesus hears the groans of the Spirit, He begins to intercede for us.
5. Jesus, knowing the will of God, begins to pray the Word of God, interceding over our wrong prayers.

In Conclusion

We, as saints of the most-high God, must learn how to pray correctly. Too often we allow our prayers to be governed by what we see and hear in the natural world. To pray correctly, take time to ask the Holy Spirit to show you what to pray and how to pray in the spirit. The Apostle Paul wrote in the 14th chapter of 1 Corinthians about praying in an unknown tongue, allowing your human spirit to pray. In doing so, you are bypassing the natural mind and understanding. He said for us to pray with all kinds of prayers and supplications in the spirit.

Note: Jesus is very familiar with the groanings from deep within, due to His being grieved as mentioned in the book of John when the people refused to believe what He said concerning Lazarus and the resurrection.

> **John 11:25** *Jesus said unto her, I am the resurrection, and the life: he that believeth in me, though he were dead, yet shall he live…*
>
> *(33) When Jesus therefore saw her weeping, and the Jews also weeping which came with her, he **groaned** in the spirit, and was troubled (agitated, disturbed, stirred up, to cause one inward commotion). (34) And said, Where have ye laid him? They said unto him, Lord, come and see. (35) Jesus wept. (36) Then said*

*the Jews, Behold how he loved him! (37) And some of them said, Could not this man, which opened the eyes of the blind, have caused that even this man should not have died? (38) Jesus therefore again **groaning in himself** cometh to the grave.*

Chapter 11

Insight on Giving Thanks

I knew what God said in all these scriptures about giving thanks, but I did not have insight as to what He was saying. As we dive into these scriptures, I will share with you what was revealed to me.

1 Thessalonians 5:18 *In everything give thanks: for this is the will of God in Christ Jesus concerning you.*

This is an easy passage to understand; it is self-explanatory. It is simply letting us know God's will for us in Christ. No matter what situation or circumstance we find ourselves in, it is God's will for us to learn how to give thanks to Him. Giving thanks to Him in the midst of a problem shifts the focus off the problem and ignites the atmosphere with praise. The only way the enemy knows if his plan is working is to watch your response. If the only reaction you have is praise amid the problem, it confuses your enemy, as he presses every button to get a negative response from you. He is watching intensely, but you refuse to indulge him. In fact, you double-crossed him; what was meant for hurt, harm, and destruction you turned into praise, spoiling the plan of the enemy.

1 Corinthians 15:57 *But thanks be to God, which giveth us the victory through our Lord Jesus Christ.*

A victory that may have not been perceived in the natural was given to you through your relentless praise and giving of thanks to God!

I understood the power and victory that I experienced when I gave God thanks **in all things**. However, I came upon a passage on giving thanks that I struggled with until I was given insight.

Ephesians 5:20 *Giving thanks always for all things unto God and the Father in the name of our Lord Jesus Christ...*

Hold on now, God!

There are some things that happened to me, things that were done to me, things that were stolen from me, things that were said about me, and God is saying to give Him thanks for them.

You must conclude the God you serve is bigger than what was done, said, happened, or stolen from you. He is so far ahead of the enemy's plans, schemes, and strategies that are designed to destroy you. When you realize this, other scriptures will begin to inspire you, such as: **Psalms 118:24** *This is the day which the Lord* (My Father) *hath made: we will rejoice and be glad in it.*

You soon understand that your Father made this day and allowed you to be in it. Everything that takes place this day or that day, Daddy God is well aware of it. Knowing this, your response is to rejoice and be glad.

Ephesians 3:13 *Wherefore I desire that ye faint not at my tribulations* (testing or trials) *for you, which is your glory.*

Hear and understand what God is saying: I don't want you to faint (wilt) at <u>my test</u> for you. In other words, it's a test that was designed for you, and God knows you can pass it. It's through these trials and tribulations that you are catapulted into another level of glory prepared just for you.

Giving Thanks to God for People

It's easy to give thanks to God for the people who have been good to you. You have nothing but wonderful memories of them.

The Apostle Paul, in his second letter to Timothy, exhorted him to pray, intercede, and **give thanks** for all men, for kings (government officials), and all who are in authority. He said, "This was acceptable in the sight of God."I'm sure there are some people we believe are not deserving of our thanks. At one time, you may have had a good relationship with them. Because of some hurts, pains, and betrayals, the last thing you want to do is to thank God for them. Listen to what the Spirit of God inspired the Apostle Paul to write:

Philippians 1:3-5 *I thank my God upon **every remembrance** of you,* (4) *Always in every prayer of mine for you all making request with joy,* (5) *For your fellowship in the gospel **from the first day unto now**...* (Emphasis mine.)

- How did the Apostle Paul remain thankful upon every remembrance?
- How did the Apostle Paul continue to pray for others with joy?
- How did he maintain it from the first day until now?

In most relationships, people are on their best behavior in the beginning stages. Everything seems to be going smoothly; we tolerate and overlook shortcomings. However, what seemed insignificant in the early stages has now resulted in division, animosity, and bad memories. Yet the Apostle Paul said, "Thanks should be given from the first day until now." The answer is found in verses 6 and 7:

Philippians 1:6 *Being confident of this very thing, that he which hath begun a good work in you will perform it until the day of Jesus Christ...*

Paul's confidence was not in the actions of others, but in the fact that **God** had begun a good work. He understood and had insight that people were in the early stages of a good work and that **God would** perform the completion of that work.

Philippians 1:7 *Even as it is meet* (beneficial) *for me to think this of you all...*

Paul realized it was to his benefit to think a certain way, no matter what others were doing or saying. The Apostle Paul captured the thoughts of God in his attitude toward others.

Act on What Has Been Revealed Part 1 (Giving Thanks / Releasing Others)

After receiving insight, we must activate what has been revealed to us. I experienced something in my ministry that caused me to wonder how I would respond when I was face-to-face with my accusers. In my mind, they had deserted me. I thought they were trying to destroy the ministry through lawsuits. The plan of the enemy failed, yet I was left with bad memories and unresolved issues. This relationship had such a good start, and four years had passed without any communication. I thank God for the separation, which allowed Him to work on me and give me insight into what He was saying through the apostle Paul. The words, from the first day until now, exploded in me, and I had to activate them.

One day, I was leaving a store with a huge parking lot, and wouldn't you know it? That person had parked right next to me. As I was about to enter my vehicle, that person was getting out of their vehicle. We briefly acknowledged one another in passing. Then the Spirit of God had me stop that person and thank her for something good she had done while serving with us in the ministry. I could tell she was surprised and somewhat startled by the words I said. I knew that something had broken in her as those words were released into her atmosphere.

As you have read this portion of this book, I pray that the Spirit of the living God will move you to give thanks for all men and destroy the works of the devil.

Chapter 12

Act on What Has Been Revealed Part 2 (God Revealed it for a Purpose)

During one of our Sunday morning church services, my wife captured a thought of God via the word of knowledge. This captured thought was something the Lord wanted to be done in that service, on that day. This occurred as she was standing on the stage with me, as the praise and worship had ended. She whispered these words to me, which caused me to pause and think, *How am I going to handle this?*

This is what she said: "The Lord said there is someone in here today who is struggling with masturbation, and he wants to set them free."

I was startled by those words, then I turned and looked over the congregation. I noticed there were some new faces in the audience that morning. I turned to my wife and said, "Oh no! That's for a Wednesday service, not Sunday."

Can you imagine the clay trying to tell the potter what day he can work?

After I said those words to my wife, she responded by saying, "I'm just telling you what the Lord said." Then she just walked away, leaving me to deal with the thoughts of God she had captured.

Wisdom to Know How to Handle a Captured Word

Capturing a thought of this nature from God requires wisdom. Again, I said *wisdom*, not **we is dumb!** As I stood on the stage alone, my prayer was, *Lord, how am I to handle this word? My wife is certain she heard from you. God, give me Your wisdom in how to handle this delicate issue.*

> **James 1:5** *If any of you lack wisdom, let him ask of God, that giveth to all men liberally, and upbraideth not; and it shall be given him.*

I knew I could not just stand up and say, "It has been revealed that someone in here is dealing with masturbation, and God wants to set you free. Who are you?"

No one would dream of responding and coming forward to a call like that. Here are the instructions the Lord gave me: He said, "Have an altar call that consists of a prayer for salvation, healing, and family issues."

I followed the instructions and about twenty people responded to the call. For the most part, they were faces with which we were familiar. My wife and I started from one end to of the prayer line, working our way to the other end. As was my normal routine, I clasped each person's hand as I softly asked what they needed prayer for today. Some needed healing, others wanted prayer for their family, and some were ready to give their life to the Lord. As we continued through the prayer line, we came face-to-face with a man we had never seen before. I took him by the hand and whispered in his ear, "Sir, what is it you need prayer for today?"

He responded, "I am having trouble with masturbation."

Momentarily, the enemy hit me with a fleshly thought as I was holding this man's hand, especially knowing the nature of that sin. The concern was for my hand, my *Holy* hand. That thought originated from the devil. When has the devil ever been concerned about holy, and besides that, there is nothing about my hand or any other part of my body that is so Holy that God can't use it to touch someone else's life. Look at Jesus's response to the leprous man.

Matthew 8:3 *And Jesus put forth his hand, and touched him, saying, I will; be thou clean. And immediately his leprosy was cleansed.*

This was not the time to bring attention to that man by praying out loud and mentioning his situation. This was the time for the Lord to show this man His love and power to deliver. We prayed and God did!

What if We Had Not Acted on that Captured Thought?

Knowing my wife, if she were reading the above question, she would probably be thinking, *What do you mean* we? So, let me rephrase, what if *I* had not acted on that captured thought?

We later found out that the man who had that problem was a teacher at one of the local Christian schools, where he also attended church.

Again, what if I had decided the thought my wife had captured was not appropriate for a Sunday morning service? I would have found myself interfering with what God wanted that day. That man may not have received his deliverance and could possibly still be bound to it today. Because of the foreknowledge of God, He knew my wife would be bold enough to say what she heard. He also knew I would be obedient. Therefore, He could send that man in whom He loved to a safe place for deliverance.

What Does God Know About You and Your Church?

These are very important questions we all should ponder:
1. What does God know about you as an individual?
2. Will you capture His thoughts?
3. What if the thought seems ridiculous? Will you receive it?
4. Will you allow fear to stop you or prevent you from speaking or acting on the thought you have captured?

NOTE: I do not pose these questions to bring out the flakes, people who are on a personal quest to show they are spiritual. No, to the contrary, I pose these questions for those who are humble yet bold before God. They are humble to the point of prayerful submission to His will and ways. At the same time, they are bold to the point where they are willing to possibly miss it while trying to make it, rather than missing out because of fear.

I Missed it Because of Fear

I can recall an incident that took place at a gas station in Wichita Falls, Texas. I often had my company vehicle serviced at this station and had become friends with the mechanic.

One day while I was standing at the cash register, the mechanic on duty grabbed his ear in extreme pain. He called out my name, then said, "My ear is hurting really bad."

Though I was a young and somewhat new believer, I captured the thought of God at that moment. I heard the words, *Pray for him audibly, openly, and I will heal him.*

I was afraid and did not do as I was instructed. I did not mention to this person that I was going to pray. What I did was pray underneath my breath, where no one could hear me. As soon as I finished, a bug came out of the man's ear, and the pain was gone. As I left the place, I heard these words in my spirit: *YOU DID NOT GLORIFY ME!*

My mental response was, *How did I not glorify you? I prayed, and the bug came out.*

He responded by saying, "I took care of the pain, but he did not know it was I Who caused that bug to come out; therefore, I was not glorified."

After hearing that explanation, I repented and asked the Lord to forgive me for allowing fear to keep me from doing things exactly the way He said to do them. I pray that this will be a learning experience for you as it was for me.

What Does God Know About Your Church?

This question is posed directly to the pastors and leaders of churches today.

1. Is your church open for God?
2. Can God interrupt your service?
3. Are you tied to your format?
4. Are you concerned about what people will think?
5. Are you open for God to make a change in someone's life?
6. Could God lead someone to your church like the man He led to ours?
7. Can your church be counted on to allow the Spirit of God to move as He pleases, when He pleases, how He pleases, and through whom He pleases?

Note: These questions are not posed for the church to be open to all kinds of crazy and weird actions. I am well aware of the crazy actions that have been and are still taking place in churches today. Some may even say they are doing things under the guise of the Holy Spirit. We must be careful that in our efforts to keep the crazy from coming in, that we don't set up man's religious walls to keep the Holy Spirit out!

Chapter 13

Our Oklahoma Assignment

In 1993, when I moved to central Oklahoma in a community east of Oklahoma City, the Lord told me to start a church. I argued with God about this commission. This area seemed to have a church on every corner. My thought was, *Lord, the last thing they need in this area is another church.* As we visited various churches in the community and its surroundings, we quickly realized what the Lord wanted from us. I heard and received a commission from the Lord Jesus specifically as to what he wanted broken in that area.

As we visited several of the churches in the area, we realized the congregations were all white or all black. In a few churches, there may be one or two black walnuts in the vanilla ice cream. (You get my drift.)

We had been members of a multi-racial church in Lawton, Oklahoma, so the makeup of these church congregations was shocking. I can recall one of the white congregations was begging us to stay and be a part of their body. I could see that some of the pastors sincerely desired a change in their congregation but did not know how to bring about that change. They were unaware of the spiritual atmosphere that bound these churches to segregation.

The Lord gave my wife and I a mandated assignment. He said, "I want to use you to break religious, racial, and gender barriers in this area."

Wouldn't you know it, after those words were spoken the devil showed up. As said in the gospels, "The enemy comes immediately to steal the word." He came at me with accusations, ones I knew were untrue, yet still they needed to be addressed.

He said to me, "How can you break down the walls of racism when you are prejudiced yourself?"

My response was I attended an interracial church. I have several friends who are white in and outside the church. Before I was saved, the friends my wife and I hung out with were of different ethnicities. A black couple, a white couple, a black woman married to a white guy, a black man married to a white woman, and white guy married to a Mexican woman. I hit him with all my credentials that should put to rest this accusation of racism he had railed against me. It wasn't really directed at me but at the assignment God had given us. I was confident that what I had spoken had to shut him up. After all, I had just released what is referred to as **a mic drop moment.** I also didn't recall him throwing out those accusations when we were partying with that multiracial group.

The Devil Is Persistent

The enemy responded to my response with something about me that appeared to be true. Knowing I like sports, he used boxing to raise his final accusation. Here's what he said, which caused me to go running back to God, asking him if He's sure I'm the one for that assignment.

Here was the accusation: "How come when you are watching boxing and it's a black boxer verses a white boxer, you are always rooting for the black guy?"

As I examined myself, it seemed that the enemy was correct. Because I found myself agreeing with my enemy, I disqualified myself from my God-given assignment. I ran to God, reciting the word of accusation that I received by agreeing with the enemy of my call. I said to God, "How can I do this? I am prejudiced." This reminds me of what happened to Adam in Genesis chapter 3 after he listened to the serpent.

God's response was amazing. (Verse 11) *Who told thee that thou wast naked?* God was saying, **"Who have you been listening to?** You did not get that information by listening to Me. You must have been eating from another tree!"

I must admit, I had been listening to the serpent and eating from the wrong tree. Because I had fallen to the subtility of the serpent, yet the assignment was still mine to carry out, God in his infinite wisdom restored me using the same line of questioning the enemy had used to bind me.

The enemy used a tree to cause man to fall, but God used a tree to bring mankind back into redemption. As Jesus was hanging on that tree *(the cross made from a tree)*, the devil thought he had won. However, God had allowed him to pick his choice of weapons. He seemed to be saying to his enemy, "If it's tree warfare you want, it's tree warfare you are going to get!"

In my case, if it's boxing warfare you want, it's boxing warfare that you are going to get.

The Question God Asked Me

Using the same analogy the devil used but with a different twist, God said, "Joe, when you are watching Olympic boxing and the white boxer represents the USA and the black boxer is representing another country, who are you rooting for?"

I responded, "The white guy!" Suddenly, something fell off me, and I said, "I'm back in the game!" My attorney Jesus via the Holy Spirit rested His case. **This was the real mic drop moment!**

Chapter 14

Lord Take Me by the Hand

Early in my ministry career, I learned that God wanted to be in control of every facet of the church service. One event took place as we were having our first church service in our first church building. Days prior to the Sunday service, we published the opening of our church in the newspaper. The Saturday before our grand opening, I had fabricated a sign with our church's name on it so everyone would know they were at Fresh Fire Church. The sign was large, and I had no way of hanging it above the door to the outside entrance. At that time, I didn't know how important hanging that sign would be. Late that evening, a friend of a friend came with the equipment needed to hang the sign. That Sunday morning, a couple arrived, and we visited with them prior to the start of the service. They told us they had seen the ad in the paper, and on Saturday morning they had tried to find the location of the church. They had the address of the building but did not see a sign out front. They waited later that evening and decided to try again. To their surprise, the sign was up on the building.

As others arrived, I preached my first message in that building. At the end of the service, I had an altar call for anyone who wanted to receive Jesus as their savior or if they just wanted prayer. That couple came up for prayer. I felt led to pray for them individually and not as a couple. I prayed for the wife first, and I watched as the Spirit of God began to minister to her as she wept. As I started to move towards her husband, intending to lay my hand on his head, the Holy Spirit stopped me. I backed up and started praying with my spirit as he had his hands lifted towards heaven. I moved forward towards him a second time with the intention of laying my hands on the man's belly. Again I was stopped by the Spirit of God, so I backed up and continued to pray with my spirit. Then I captured the thought of God. I was instructed to take both of my hands and hit him on both of his hands at the same time. As the man's hands were lifted in the air, I did as I was instructed, and the power of God hit that man and knocked him to the floor. He laid there weeping as God was working on him.

After the service was over, the man came to me and said, "As I was standing in the prayer line with my hands upraised, I was saying to God, 'If you are real, take me by the hands.' The next thing I knew, something hit my hands and I ended up on the floor."

It was then that I realized why the Lord would not allow me to pray for this man as I had intended. The scripture says, "We are laborers together with God." Therefore, it is important that we do things His way and we will get His results.

Chapter 15

Praying, Speaking and Releasing in the Spirit (The Breaking of a Stronghold)

There are so many things we may be warring for and against. We are often praying for a release of things to us that the Lord Jesus said, **have been** freely given to us. At the same time, we must stand against the attacks of the enemy whose only intent is to kill, steal, and destroy. Natural things are being held from us due to strangleholds of the spirits in heavenly places.

As we, along with a few others, began to walk in our God-given assignment in the assigned area, after about three years we began to see the fruits of our labor. At the same time, we warred in the realm of spirit, commanding the spirit of racism to come down from its high place. As Paul said in **Ephesians 6:12,** *For we wrestle not against flesh and blood, but against principalities, against powers, against the rulers of the darkness of this world, against spiritual wickedness **in high places.*** (Emphasis mine.)

We watched as people both black and white began to enter our church. Then the Spirit of God placed on my heart a compassion for black and white couples. At that time, in that area, churches were not open to people coming together who were on the opposite ends of the color spectrum. In our church's puppet ministry, we had a set of black and white puppets that were a married couple. They were the point of contact, used to stand in the gap until we had received the manifestation for what we were praying. As we warred in that area, against the forces of darkness, that too had to bow its knee to the Lord Jesus. Our congregation of both blacks and whites were now worshipping the Lord together.

A Divided Church

As our church began to grow, I began to glory in what God was doing. One Sunday morning as I was preaching, I noticed the church was divided. Although we were praying, praising, and worshipping together, we were still divided. The Blacks were on one side and the Whites were on the other. Families and friends were coming and sitting together. I knew this had happened innocently, but I also knew this needed to be addressed. I couldn't tell people who they could sit with or where they could sit. I again needed the wisdom of God. I knew if I could capture His thought, I would have His wisdom. The thought I captured was to allow the people to see as I was seeing. If they were to look at the audience from my perspective, what would they see? I posed that question, and the people immediately began to see. Sunday after Sunday, the seating arrangements began to change.

Envied and Attacked

As our church began to grow, some of our white church families began to say, "Pastor, can you believe I was asked, why I am going to that black church?"

The church was mixed now. However, in the eyes and minds of some, the face of the church is based on the color of the pastor. As a matter of fact, when I first started the ministry, the only black family was my own.

The accusations toward us began to swirl from both the black churches and the white churches. They said things like, "They are stilling sheep." Not many wanted to fellowship with us. We would support their events, but they remained absent from ours. We were not moved, for we understood the source of the attack was not man, but of the powers of darkness.

Another Stronghold Must Come Down

Our church continued to grow and rejoice in how God had broken the color barrier. It wasn't long before the Spirit of God began to deal with another ethnic stronghold that needed to come down. I was raised in Kansas City, Missouri until I was twenty, then I moved to Wichita Falls, Texas and lived there for 14 years. I don't remember having any interactions with Native Americans. However, in our area of Oklahoma, there were several different tribes. I noticed that they too were segregated. For the most part, they worshipped in their own way amongst their own tribes.

Once I attended a Native American wake / funeral service. The people began to moan and utter songs in their tribal language. I did not understand the words; however, the sounds, tones, and frequency was like what I had heard in the old Black Baptist and Pentecostal churches. Little did I know that God was opening doors that would give me a platform, a way to connect with my Native American brothers and sisters. I should have picked up on it when we purchased our home. All the streets in the housing community were named after Native American tribes.

My Meeting with a Tribal Chief

One time, the building we were having our services in was sold out from under us. We began to hold our church services in a hotel room, carrying sound equipment back and forth in the dead of winter. The children had to walk past the salad bar to get to the room where they would have their services. Week after week, month after month, we continued, as I searched for a permanent building. I noticed some members began to get restless. One of the ladies said to me, "Pastor, I don't do hotel church, and I'm not coming back until you get us a real church building!"

You may think those were some hard words, and they were! At least I knew where she stood. This lady was true to her word. She left then returned when we found a church building.

Note: While under pressure to find a building, I almost signed a rental contract that would have ruined our church financially. (I said almost.) A Word to the wise: NEVER MAKE A DECISION UNDER PRESSURE!

After a long search, we finally found the building God wanted for us, the one a prophet had seen in a vision that would seat 500 and had an upstairs. As I researched to find who the owner was, I learned it was owned by one of the local tribes. I set up a meeting and they allowed some of my leaders and I to view this church that they had intended to use as a daycare. As we walked through the building, we knew this was it. There was an old handwritten sign over the entrance into the sanctuary that read "Occupancy 500."

The next step was how to rent this building. We had to do much praying in the Spirit, for some tribal members were opposed to us renting the building and selling was not even an option. As we continued to pray, somehow we scheduled a meeting for me to meet the chief of the tribe. As I arrived at the tribal office, I told the secretary I had a scheduled meeting with the chief.

She said, "He is in a tribal council meeting and will meet with you afterward."

As I waited, I studied the native American paintings, portraits, and cultural artifacts that were hanging on the walls of the waiting area. My stare was suddenly interrupted by the secretary.

With boldness she said, "The Chief will see you now!"

I started walking, with wobbly legs that reminded me of the scarecrow as he was going before the great Oz. As I sat before the chief, I did not introduce myself as Pastor Joe. I explained to him the purpose of my visit.

His immediate response was, "Sir, you could have saved yourself a lot of time if you had called me. I would have told you over the phone that the tribal council is not interested in selling, leasing, or renting that building."

I didn't know what to say to him after that. I had been told by a tribal member not to say anything that may be offensive to the chief. He may not be open to all that "Jesus stuff." The thought I captured in my spirit was that I needed to mention Jesus, and I did! I told him how the Lord Jesus had led us to that church and the prophetic signs that he had given us.

To my surprise, he responded back with these words: "You want to know something? About three months ago I gave my life to the Lord Jesus."

For the next hour we talked about Jesus, and as I was leaving his office he said, "I'm going to take your matter before the council myself."

He did as he said, and we gained access to that church. Even today, the chief and I remain friends. Glory to God!

Access to More Than a Church Building

God doesn't always tell us the complete story. We must learn to trust Him like the saints of old. As Genesis 17 said, Abraham was told by God to get from amongst his kinfolk, out of his father's house and *I will make you a father of many nations.*

In **Acts 9:6**, in his encounter with Jesus, the Apostle Paul said, "Lord what wilt thou **have me to do**?" (Emphasis mine.)

Jesus responded by saying, "Arise, and go into the city, and it shall be told thee what thou **must do**." (Emphasis mine.)

The first step will often lead or send you into the direction of the next step that God has for you.

Earlier I mentioned there were more strongholds that needed to come down. Through all the things that had happened to us, God's plan was starting to unfold. These things were not merely coincidental; they were revealing a greater plan by a great God. Meeting the chief and occupying that building was a gateway into something much deeper. As we gained access to the church building, the first order of business was to establish which of the rooms would be the prayer room / war room. After much prayer, the Lord gave me some specific instructions: Instead of having one night of prayer, we were to divide into two groups. One group would be called the "Special Forces." They were assigned to pray in the Spirit and get information and share it with the second group. On the second day of prayer, we would all pray and conduct spiritual warfare collectively. Everyone wanted to be a part of that first group, probably because of the name the Special Forces, but we dealt with that spirit of division. The Spirit of God handpicked the ones who were to be a part of the first group, men and women who could keep rank and follow spiritual instructions. After praying and doing as we were instructed, we finally started praying in the Spirit with the Spirit.

Tongues Transcending Dialects

One night as I was praying with the first team, our prayer language began to change at the same time. We were all praying with the same volume, the same tone, and the same frequency. We had reached a place in the Spirit where we were praying in a Native American dialect. We found ourselves warring in that dialect, giving commands like a chief would do. We were commanding certain demonic strongholds to come down. We started taking authority over the spirit of the medicine man and of witchcraft. Specific things were revealed to us that we took back to the second team on the next prayer night. As the second prayer night came, I told the team what had happened and what had been revealed. I told them we needed them to war with us in the Spirit and they did. As we prayed together with our spirit, we reentered that state and released words in that same dialect. Not only did we war, but we broke through to releasing worship songs to the Lord in the very same Native American dialect.

The Stronghold Was Broken

We knew we had broken through and the stronghold that had kept our Native American brothers and sisters in this area isolated from the church was broken. We immediately began to see the fruit of our labor as we watched Native American families make their way into the church. Our church was now mixed with Blacks, Whites, and Native Americans. What God started in the late 1990's had blossomed into several interracial churches of all denominations in this area today. What some area pastors had cried out to God for, which seemed to be impossible, is now in full manifestation. Thanks be to God Who always causes us to triumph in Christ Jesus. Mission accomplished!!!!!

Culture Differences and Racial Divides

When pastoring or dealing with people of multiple races, it is important to understand another component called culture. If you are not aware of this, the enemy will use cultural differences disguised as racism as a gateway for division and separation. There are some things that are said and done in one culture that may be acceptable in that culture but offensive in another.

One day we invited some members of our church to our house for cake. We had not yet pulled any utensils out to cut the cake. One of my sons who had an Afro, happened to be walking around with an Afro rake stuck in his hair. This rake was also referred to as a "cake cutter."

When one of the ladies from a different nationality saw it, she said, "Why is he walking around with that in his hair?" She began to be offended because she thought we were going to use that cake cutter to cut the cake. In their culture, they did use that instrument for cutting cakes. That is what it was originally designed for.

It would be beneficial for us as pastors and leaders to be aware of Satan's plan to use cultural differences as a doorway for division. Certain words can be offensive to others if the enemy has his way.

When your people know your heart, they will understand your words!

Chapter 16

In My Church and Home but Not in My Family

If we are going to bring real and true change into our churches, we must have real and true change in our hearts. If we have the slightest prejudice, I can assure you, it will eventually be exposed. The Spirit of God wants to expose it or make it known to us in advance. He wants to make it known to us privately before the enemy exploits it publicly.

I witnessed this in a church I once attended. This was a good church, with a great pastor. The church congregation was totally interracial and had people from several different ethnicities. We worshipped together, ate together, and hung out together after church services were over. We hugged and embraced one another, referring to each other as brothers and sisters. The relationships all seemed to be so wonderful. Then something happened that exposed the hidden issues in the hearts of certain leaders in our church body. The enemy could use this issue to fragment and divide some of the relationships.

There was a young man who often fellowshipped with one particular family. Although this young man was a different race from that family, they would introduce him as their son. He seemed to fit in with their sons and daughters without any problems. After a while, the older daughter and the young man started to have feelings for each other. The girl's parents became aware of the relationship and made them break up. It wasn't because they had done anything wrong; the issue was color. Questions arose such as, how would the relatives feel about this relationship? All sorts of excuses and concerns came out as to why this was forbidden. However, the truth was race, which revealed their hypocrisy. As the news of this filtered through the church, so did that spirit work its way in also. This remains a plague in our churches today, a hidden issue of the heart, that secretly says, "I accept you in my church, even in my home, **but not in my family!**"

Leaders Must Address Leaders

Something happened in a church I attended in my youth in Kansas City, Missouri. When I went to visit this church with my family, I was disturbed by the words being said from the pulpit.

As the pastor was preaching **his message,** he continued saying, "The white man is doing this, and the white man is doing that."

Knowing I was to be an instrument of God to bring about unity, I knew I must address this issue with the pastor.

My question was, "Lord, how would You want me to address this?" Again, *I captured the thought of God*; therefore, I had the wisdom of God.

He told me what to say and presented me with an opportunity to privately speak with the pastor. After the service was over, the pastor recognized who I was and invited me into his office.

Here is what I was to say: "Pastor, you said some things in your message about white people. I know you didn't mean any harm, but would you feel comfortable saying those things if you had white people in your church? How would they feel? Do you know that God *does* want to send whites to your church?"

He recognized what he was saying was not right and thanked me for bringing it to his attention.

So often people think they can get away with saying things and making racial remarks in our churches or in private meetings. They may feel it's safe to say certain things because of the color of their audience. For the most part, they have gotten away with those remarks because no one confronts them. If things like this go unchecked, there will be no real and true change in our churches or in society and hypocrisy will be allowed to continue.

The Apostle Paul addressed the Apostle Peter for his hypocrisy. This had to be dealt with specifically because it came from church leadership and others were being impacted by it. We must capture God's thoughts on these issues and allow Him to show us how and when to address them.

Galatians 2:11 *But when Peter was come from Antioch, I withstood him to the face, because he was to be blamed* (at fault).

Chapter 17

Don't Get Stuck on Tongues (A Captured Thought)

O ne morning as I was listening to a prayer call, I heard in my spirit the words, *Don't get stuck on tongues!* As I pondered those words, I knew the Holy Spirit would give me insight. So often we hear words, but do we understand what God is trying to convey? With that phrase stuck in my spirit, I knew I had captured a thought of God. Now that God had my attention, I was open to hear what the Holy Spirit wanted to reveal.

My People Are Getting Stuck on Tongues

Isn't it amazing that God is concerned about the things that impact His people? One might think that God's concern is with those who refuse to accept the use of tongues in the lives of believers today. But that doesn't seem to be His major concern based on what I hear in my spirit. You might think that unbelieving Christians are the top priority, but that is not the case.

Romans 3:3 *For what if some did not believe? shall their unbelief make the faith of God without effect?*

What makes the Word of God of no effect is the traditions of man. (**Mark 7:13**)

Tongues Stuck by the Traditions of Man

Growing up among Pentecostals, I witnessed several things in the church that would cause most Christians to ask, "Is this biblical?" From what I witnessed, there had to be some type of hype before an utterance in tongues was released. The praise music had to be going, the sound of the drums, piano, and guitars must be playing. Excitement seemed to fill the atmosphere, then some in the group would utter a few words in a language that no one understood. This seemed to be a tradition created by man as to what kind of atmosphere was needed before an utterance in tongues. As this happened repeatedly, it opened the door for a tradition of man to be established. The excitement of music and spectacular preaching was the portal by which tongues were accepted in the church. Unknowingly, this tradition of man passed from church to church.

Tongues Stuck by Familiarity

Have you ever noticed that some Christians use the same few words in their prayer language over and over again? No matter what we may be praying for, the same exact words seem to come out of their mouths. I often wonder how could those same exact few words cover every situation or every prayer request? What I now understand is that they are familiar with those few words. They may have been the words they first received when they were filled with the Holy Ghost. Can you imagine trying to communicate with people using the same three to four words? You would be very limited in what you could accomplish, and frustration would be inevitable.

When I was first filled with the Holy Spirit and spoke my first words in tongues, I could use only a few words. However, the more I prayed, the more fluent I became. One of the reasons some may be stuck is the environment that they are in will not allow them to move beyond familiarity.

Therefore, their tongues are stuck due to familiarity.

Startup Tongues

So many Spirit-filled, tongue-talking believers seem to use the same words when they start to pray but never move beyond those few words. Then I heard in my spirit the words, *startup tongues*. I captured that thought. Once a thought is captured, insight comes next. Insight will give an explanation using examples of something you can comprehend. Insight examples do not promote confusion nor cloud the captured thought of God. You may ask, "How can I know I have captured the thought of God?" Let me remind you of what we discussed earlier. There are three sources of thoughts: the thoughts of man, the thoughts of satan, and the thoughts of God. The thoughts of God will always advance His kingdom agenda.

Startup Tongues Explanation

Most of us will be able to identify with this example: when you start a combustible engine, if you listen, you will notice a difference in the cranking sound. Each make has a unique startup sound. Whether made by Ford, Chevy, Chrysler, or Buick, the cranking sound their engines make is distinctly and uniquely different. Under normal situations, whenever their engine starts, it creates the same sound. This is an example of when the natural mimics the spiritual.

Stuck in Startup

When it comes to driving our vehicles, we must first start the engine. This phrase was often mentioned prior to auto races: "Gentlemen, start your engines!" When the engine has been started, it releases a totally different sound. The tone, the volume, and the frequency change as the accelerator is pressed. These vehicles are now ready for sudden movement that will carry them to the finish line.

What would happen if the engine failed to start?

If the engine failed to start, we would realize we were going nowhere. We would understand that our movement had stopped; we would be stuck in startup mode. As we continued to crank the engine, the only sound it would make was the startup sound. This is going on in the lives of many spirit-filled believers. Don't allow yourself to be stuck in startup, releasing the same sound. My prayer today, as you have read this section, is that something stirs inside you, such a stirring in your spirit that you will spend more time in prayer, allowing the Holy Spirit to release to you an expansion of the language of tongues.

The Language of Tongues

Those who are opposed to speaking in tongues often say, "You're just speaking gibberish!" They refuse to acknowledge this is a language, whether they understand it or not! What's even more alarming is that those who do speak with other tongues have yet to understand it is a language.

If you do not understand that this is a language and not just an utterance, you are missing out on its true value and use. When you speak in your natural language, your volume, tone, and frequency may change depending on the situation at hand. It sounds different when you are happy to see someone. Your words may convey great excitement. Maybe you are at a sporting event, and you are cheering for your team. Maybe you are on a stage and giving a speech, or you may be asking someone a question. There are times when you may aggressively deal with an issue. There are times when you are calmly and softly conversing with others. These are examples of the use of your language. Again, the situation or event will dictate the volume, tone, and frequency of the words you speak to bring about the desired results. Your native language is spoken in variations of sounds from low to high frequency, from soft to loud, and from fast to slow. Why is this so important? It is very important to understand that these uses of your natural language are normal.

As the Natural so Is the Spiritual

I have laid out before you the normal use of your natural language. Your spiritual language is the same. Some may say within themselves, "I have arrived; I am fluent in tongues." So often in prayer, we release the same sound, the same volume, the same tone, and the same frequency. We have become monotone (unchanging in pitch and tone) in our prayer language. Perhaps we fail to recognize we are speaking in a language.

A Volume, Tone, and Frequency Change

Sometimes when I am praying in the Spirit, with my spirit, my volume, tone, and frequency may change. This change is based on what and to whom I am addressing. Sometimes my speaking in tongues may become aggressive. This aggression is due to the warfare in which I may be engaged. There are other times God may be using my tongue to give commands in the spirit realm which constitutes a change in sound. Sometimes I am rejoicing in my spirit, which releases a different sound. The sound I release to God, which so pleases Him, is the sound of worship.

Listen to what the Apostle Paul wrote about sounds and their importance.

> **1 Corinthians 14:7, 8** *And even things without life giving sound, whether pipe or harp, except they give a distinction* (difference, variation) *in the sounds, how shall it be known what is piped or harped? (8) For if the trumpet give an uncertain* (hidden, uncertain) *sound, who shall prepare himself for the battle?*

> **1 Corinthians 14:10** *There are, it may be, so many kinds of voices* (sounds, tones, and tongues) *in the world, and none of them is without signification* (voiceless, meaning).

Tongues of Aggression

I mentioned earlier that I may pray with tongues of aggression. I want to be clear: I never pray or release tongues of aggression toward God. When I come before Him, my volume, tone, and frequency changes to complete humility and adoration. For I know that He is God, and I am man, made in His image and likeness.

My aggression is directed toward the kingdom of darkness that is trying to keep me from receiving the things Jesus has freely prepared for me. Yes, we must be aggressive in that warfare.

Matthew 11:12 *And from the days of John the Baptist until now the kingdom of heaven suffereth violence, and the violent take it by force.*

Chapter 19

Speaking in the Spirit

The Apostle Paul mentioned the words, *in the Spirit*, when he addressed the early church's venture into the spiritual. For the most part, that term has been limited to or associated with praying in tongues. Could there be something more or a much deeper meaning in those words?

Paul said something else in his letter to the church in Galatia. He shared that he had received revelation (revealed knowledge) from the Lord Jesus. He wrote about things that were inspired by the Holy Spirit. When it came to the gospel and spiritual things, Paul said, *"For I neither received it from man, nor was I taught it, but I received it through a revelation of Jesus Christ."*

Here are two passages of scripture where Paul used the words, *in the spirit*. The first is in reference to the use and misuse of tongues in the church by the church. **1 Corinthians 14:1, 2** *Follow after charity, and desire spiritual gifts, but rather that ye may prophesy. (2) For he that speaketh in an unknown tongue speaketh not unto men but unto God: for no man understandeth him; howbeit in the spirit he speaketh mysteries.*

The second referred to spiritual warfare, as he wrote to the believers in the church of Ephesus. **Ephesians 6:18** *Praying always with all prayer and supplication **in the Spirit** and watching thereunto with all perseverance and supplication for all saints…* (Emphasis mine.)

As we know, the Word of God is alive, living and breathing; therefore, it is packed with hidden truths. Let us unpack the words, *in the spirit he speaketh mysteries.* Paul revealed a hidden truth, that with our spirit, we can speak and release words into the realm of the spirit. This takes place when you are praying with the Spirit, and you enter the atmosphere of the Spirit. Sometimes when you worship, your pure, genuine worship to God elevates you into a different realm in the spirit. In this atmosphere, the spiritual takes precedent over the natural. The Spirit of God is in control, and you need not speak anything. This is totally the opposite of the hidden truth when the Holy Spirit uses you to speak and release into the atmosphere. In that realm, we command the spirits of darkness to come under the subjection of the Word of God!

In the Spirit and with my Spirit

In the spirit may not always refer to what one is speaking but to the realm in which one is speaking. There is a natural realm and a spiritual realm. With our natural senses, we contact the natural realm, but we contact the spirit realm with our spirits. For us to pray or speak in the realm of the spirit, we must first enter that realm. It is our spirit not our natural man that engages the spiritual. So, it is with our spirit that we can speak and pray in the atmosphere of the spirit. As believers, our spirit is the only part of man that has the ability via the Holy Spirit to access the spiritual atmosphere. Notice, I used the words praying and speaking, for they are totally different words. The Apostle Paul, in his effort to correct and bring order to the use of tongues in the church, mentioned these two words:

Speaketh: *(laleo / lal-eh'-0) to make sounds, to talk, to utter words, to preach or proclaim.*

Pray: *(proseuchomai / pro-yoo-khom-ahee) to offer prayer, to pray to God, to offer supplication and worship.*

The terms "speaking in tongues" and "speaking with my spirit" can be used interchangeably, as Paul often did. However, speaking in tongues or with the spirit is not the same as *in* the spirit. You must understand this: tongues is what you are speaking with. However, *"in* *the spirit" represents **where** you are speaking.* It depicts the atmosphere in which you are releasing words.

There are times, when in the spirit, you are having a God conversation. Other times you are engaged in spiritual warfare, where you are authoritatively releasing the Word of God into heavenly places. You may be giving commands for things to be released from one atmosphere into another. You may be demanding a release of people, places, and things. These are all which have been held captive by the enemy. Keep in mind you are demanding of the enemy, not of God! So many things have been held in captivity because the church has no understanding of the terms, *with* our spirit and *in* the spirit. In doing so, we have failed to speak that which is a mystery (that which is hidden) into the spiritual realm to bring about the necessary earthly changes.

We must understand when we are speaking *with* our spirit, we are not always speaking *in* the spirit. Both Paul and Jude alluded to the fact that tongues can also be used to edify (build up) oneself, and we do that when we are not speaking in the spirit.

Praying with the Spirit

As believers, when we are praying with our spirit, we are never praying to the devil. We should never ask the enemy for anything. We are not looking to him for any of our provisions. Never at any time when we are praying with our spirit, are our prayers directed to Satan or ourselves. Whether with our spirit or with our understanding, the target for our prayers is the throne of the Most High God.

We can be assured when we are praying, singing, or giving thanks with our spirit, we are doing well, as said by the Apostle Paul:

1 Corinthians 14:17 *For thou verily **givest thanks well**, but the other is not edified.* (Emphasis mine.)

My Spirit Prayeth

1 Corinthians 14:14A *For if I pray in an unknown tongue, my spirit prayeth…*

Most people would agree that when praying, the use of the tongue is an important component to release sounds which form words. When we pray in a known tongue, we are uttering words which originated from our minds. This is quite different when we are praying with our spirit. When I have been praying in tongues or with my spirit there have been times that I was interrupted. I stopped praying to address something or to talk to someone. What was so fascinating is that when I stopped praying outwardly, prayer was still going on inside my spirit. I could still hear tongues being released deep within my inward man. The bible declares there is an inward and an outward man.

2 Corinthians 4:16b *…but though our outward man perish, yet the inward man is renewed day by day.*

When I stopped speaking outwardly, the inward man continued speaking outwardly. Only I could hear those words, for they originated in my spirit. After I finished addressing things in the natural, I was instantly able to reconnect in prayer with my spirit and we continued together in the inward and the outward. Here is something that is very important: although these words were being released in my spirit, they were not being released until my tongue was used. God wants you to use your tongue to release what originates from within your spirit, but you must speak the words. Even on the day of Pentecost, words were released but they had to speak them.

Acts 2:4 *And **they** were all filled with the Holy Ghost, and **began to speak** with other tongues, as **the Spirit gave them the utterance.*** (Emphasis mine.)

Remember, the spoken words were given by the Spirit. It also said they began, which means that this was the start and not the end. I honestly believe that if people were taught and understood the terminology, "my spirit prayeth" they would no longer be opposed to something that is so beneficial to them. The enemy has made the words "speaking in tongues" taboo. Maybe it would be wiser to use the words, "praying with the spirit."

Chapter 20

The Three Atmospheres

From what has been written in the scriptures, we know there are three atmospheres that are also referred to as heavens. Isaiah's writing seems to support that there is more than one atmosphere:

Isaiah 14:13 & 14 *For thou hast said in thine heart,* **I will ascend into heaven,** *I will exalt my throne* **above the stars of God.** *I will sit also upon the mount of the congregation, in the sides of the north:* (14) *I will ascend* **above the heights of the clouds***; I will be like the most High.* (Emphasis mine.)

I highlighted key words to bring special attention to them. Here is a question we must ask: If Lucifer had to ascend to heaven, where was his throne or place of rule before? According to verse 14, it must have been somewhere between the earth's atmosphere and the clouds and the stars, therefore signifying that God's throne had to been beyond those heavens.

Listen to what the Apostle Paul wrote about his "caught up" experience:

2 Cor. 12:2 *I knew a man in Christ above fourteen years ago, (whether in the body, I cannot tell; or whether out of the body I cannot tell: God knoweth:) such an one was* **caught up to the third heaven.** (Emphasis mine.)

From this scripture, we can clearly see that there are three heavens, as mentioned by Paul: the heavens that are right above us, the heavens that are above the cloud and stars, and the last is the heavens where God's throne resides. In **Psalms 68:33**, David mentioned praises that should be "sung unto him that rideth upon the heavens of heavens."

Deuteronomy 10:14 *Behold, the heaven and the heaven of heavens is the Lord's...*

There are several bible references to the heavens and heavens of heavens and the spirit beings that exist in those atmospheres. Paul said we would contend with spiritual wickedness in heavenly places.

The Three Heavens / Atmospheres of Release

Now that we have clearly and biblically established that there are three heavens or atmospheres, we may proceed deeper. As the Apostle Paul said, the *yea, the deep things of God* (**1 Corinthians 2:10**).

In the first heaven / atmosphere in which we live, we can pray **with our spirit.** In doing so, we build up and edify ourselves as written in Jude verse 20: *But ye, beloved, building up yourselves on your most holy faith,* **praying in the Holy Ghost***...* (Emphasis mine.)

1 Corinthians 14:4 *He that speaketh in an unknown tongue edifieth* (builds up, restores, establish) *himself...*

As a young spirit-filled believer, it came into my heart and another brother's heart, Calvin, to preach in the streets. We were led to a place called The Faith City Mission, in Wichita Falls, Texas. The founder, Brother Pete, opened a door of opportunity to us. Two days a month, we preached in the chapel and shared the gospel with all the street people prior to them eating. We were young and excited, for this was our first opportunity. On our first day, we arrived to find several unhappy and upset people who did not like the idea of having to listen to us preach before they were allowed to eat. If you could see the looks on their faces! They gave us looks of *hurry up*, for we were standing in the way of them eating, and they were not happy campers to say the least. Some would interrupt with vulgarity and obscenity. This was our first day, and we were immediately faced with this level of opposition. However, we were not moved. Why? We understood we had to operate in what we knew, and we did. We started praying with our spirit, revving the engine, and building ourselves up.

It didn't take long, as we were emboldened and released the word of God. Some came forward and received Christ as their personal savior on that first day.

The Second Heavens

The second heaven is the atmosphere from which Satan and his cohorts operate. This is his place of rule over the world system. Let me remind you of what the Apostle Paul said about Satan:

> **2 Corinthians 4:4** *In whom **the god of this world**, hath blinded the minds of them which believe not...* (Emphasis mine.)

This world system is run by man but ruled by Satan, the god of this system. He exalts people into positions of leadership who will not oppose his dark agenda. Look at what he said to Jesus as he took Him up an exceedingly high mountain.

> **Luke 4:6** *And the devil said unto him* (Jesus), *All this power **will I give** thee, and the glory of them: for that **is delivered unto me; and to whomsoever I will I give it.*** (Emphasis mine.)

Several hidden truths must be unpacked in this one passage of scripture. First, it appears that the devil is boasting to Jesus about all the power and the glory of that power that he has under his control. He also seems to think that Jesus is in a weakened state of mind, and He may be vulnerable to the temptation of earthly glory. He also reveals that all this power that he now has was delivered to him. If all that power was delivered to him, then it wasn't his from the beginning. That being true, who delivered this power into the hands of the devil? This transfer of power took place when Adam committed high treason against God in the garden of Eden. He relinquished all the authority that God had given him from the beginning of creation. When the devil said he would give this power and glory to Jesus, if He would bow down and worship, Jesus never said, "It's not yours to give." Not one time did Jesus say, "It doesn't belong to you!" Why? Because Satan acquired it legally through subtlety (craftiness, trickery, and cunningness).

What he said that impacts believers the most is this, *to whomsoever I will I give it.*

This is the reason we find ourselves in constant warfare! This is the reason you may have been passed over in that promotion or that position! Positioning is very important when it comes to warfare. This is the atmosphere and the heavens in which we must **pray with our spirit, in the spirit** (in this realm of the spirit). This second heaven is the realm where we are to release the Word of God to have the change take place in the first heavens.

If you read Daniel chapter 10, you will see Daniel praying words that were heard and caused a war to take place in the heavens. I believe this warfare between God's messenger angel and the prince over the kingdom of Persia took place in the second heavens. The warfare was so intense that Michael, God's warring angel, had to come help the messenger angel. Michael came from the third heavens into the second heavens to assist in the battle. This battle predated Jesus coming to the earth and taking back the authority that Adam had lost. Jesus proclaimed to his followers these important words:

Matthew 28:18 *All power is given unto me in heaven and in earth.*

That battle predated His coming and the dispensation of the church being empowered by the Holy Ghost. When the Apostles asked Jesus about kingdom restoration, He replied about kingdom authority and power:

Acts 1:8 *But ye shall receive power, after that the Holy Ghost has come unto you…*

Now that we have access to war in the second heavens, the access is via **praying with your spirit, in the spirit!**

Ephesians 6:12 *For we wrestle not against flesh and blood, but against principalities, against powers, against the rulers of the darkness of this world, against spiritual wickedness in high places.*

The Third Heavens

The third heavens seem to be the place of God's rule and dominion. Access must be granted prior to entry. One cannot access this atmosphere by themselves; they must be ushered in. Paul said, "he was caught up to the third heaven," which he instantly referred to as paradise. In the third heaven, he heard words that were unspeakable. He heard words that were not spoken, yet he heard them. This helps us understand how we can hear words beyond our natural hearing. As Paul entered that realm, the Lord Jesus downloaded an abundance of revelation into his spirit.

As you probably noticed, most of my scriptural references come from the Apostle Paul's writings. Paul speaks of spiritual things that none of the other apostles even mention. Paul speaks from what was downloaded to him, revealed knowledge. Revelation gives birth to revelation. As you read some of the things written in this book, you may think, *I have never heard this nor seen that in the bible, although I have read this scripture several times before.* When revelation is released, revelational people realize from where it originates. When Peter was speaking from revelation knowledge, Jesus was well aware, as He replied, "Flesh and blood has not revealed this unto you but my father which is in heaven."

So many things have been written about the third heavens that it would take a separate book to unfold them. (Another book, another time!)

Chapter 21

Insight into the Spiritual

1 Corinthians 12:1-11 Important facts about these passages of scripture:

1. God doesn't want us to be ignorant concerning the spiritual or spiritual gifts. (1 Corinthians 12:1)
2. No one speaking by the Spirit of God will say anything that brings shame or devalues the Lord Jesus. When the Holy Spirit is in operation, He will always promote the Lordship of Jesus. (1 Corinthians 12:3)
3. The Holy Spirit oversees the gifts. That is why we refer to them as the gifts of the Spirit. (1 Corinthians 12:4)
4. Jesus oversees the administration (ministry) offices. (1 Corinthians 12:5 *"The same Lord"*) **Ephesians 4:11** says, *"And he (Jesus) gave some, apostles; and some, prophets; and some, evangelists; and some, pastors and teachers…"*
5. Whether they are the gifts of the Spirit or the five-fold ministry, God oversees their operation and how they operate. (1 Corinthians 12:6)
6. When the Spirit is in manifestation, He will produce gain and profit for the Kingdom of God. (1 Corinthians 12:7)
7. There are nine gifts of the Spirit and five ministerial offices. The nine gifts of the Spirit are: the word of **wisdom**, the word of **knowledge**, **discerning** of spirits, the gifts of **healing**, the

working of **miracles**, **faith**, *divers* kinds of **tongues**, the **interpretation** of tongues, and **prophecy**. (By the same spirit 1 Corinthians 12:8-10)

The five ministry gifts that are referred to as ministerial offices are: **Apostles, Prophets, Evangelists, Pastors, and Teachers.** (Ephesians 4:11)

The Gifts of the Spirit can be separated into three categories:

1. **Revelational Gifts (they reveal something):** the word of wisdom, the word of knowledge, and discerning of spirits.
2. **Inspirational Gifts (they say something):***Divers* kinds of tongues, the interpretation of tongues, and prophecy.
3. **The Power Gifts (they do something):** the working of miracles, the gift of healing, and the gift of faith.

The Revelational Gifts of the Spirit

Gifts of the Spirit refers to everything in the realm of knowing facts, events, purpose, origin, or destiny. Whether human, divine, devilish, natural, supernatural, past, present, or future, it will all be revealed through the manifestation of one of these gifts.

The Word of Knowledge

Definition: *A supernatural revelation by the Spirit of God. Concerning facts in the mind of God, that deal with people, places, or things. It is the supernatural revelation of things that are or have been. The word of knowledge can come via dreams, visions, tongues and the interpretation of tongues, angels, the Lord Jesus, and the Holy Spirit.*

Note: The word of knowledge will always reveal facts about the past and present. It is not called the gift of knowledge. A person doesn't receive this because of their educational status.

Scriptural Examples of the Word of Knowledge

2 Kings 6:9 Elijah through the word of knowledge revealed to the King of Israel where the Syrian soldiers were located.

As Jesus talked with the Samaritan woman at Jacob's well, through the word of knowledge He reveals her past marital status and her present relationship.

> **John 4:18** *For thou hast **had five husbands**; and he whom thou **now hast** is not thy husband...* (Emphasis mine.)

In **Luke 2:8-18,** the angel of the Lord revealed the birth and birthplace of baby Jesus to the shepherds. The angel also revealed that the child would be wrapped in swaddling clothes and lying in a manger.

In **Acts 5:1-10,** Peter by the word of knowledge knew that Ananias and his wife Sapphira were lying about how much they sold their land for.

In **Acts 9:10,** Ananias through a vision received a word of knowledge, a supernatural revelation concerning a man named Saul. In the revelation, he was giving Saul's name, location, and what he was presently doing.

In **Acts 10:5,** Cornelius received a word of knowledge to send men to Joppa, ask for a man called Simon whose surname is Peter, and lodge with a tanner named Simon whose house is by the seaside.

In **Acts 10:18, 19,** the Spirit revealed to Peter that there were three men at the door, and they were sent from God.

The Word of Wisdom

Definition: *A supernatural revelation by the Spirit of God concerning divine purposes or plans in the mind of God. It is the supernatural revelation of events that have yet to take place. The word of wisdom can also come via dreams, visions, tongues and interpretation of tongues, angels, the Lord Jesus, and the Holy Spirit.*

Note: The word of wisdom always **reveals facts about the future**. It is not the gift of wisdom; one does not receive this because of their educational status. This is not man's wisdom nor is this the wisdom King Solomon requested from God.

James 1:5 *If any of you lack wisdom, let him ask of God, that* **giveth to all men** *liberally, and upbraideth not; and it shall be given him.* (Emphasis mine.)

1 Corinthians 12:8 *For to* **one** *is given by the Spirit the word of wisdom... (Emphasis mine.)*

As you can see, the word of wisdom is clearly different from Godly wisdom, which aids with issues and answers. Not everyone operates in the word of wisdom, for it is as the Spirit wills.

Scriptural Example of the Word of Wisdom

In **Acts 9:12**, Paul saw in a vision Ananias coming and laying his hands on him so that he might receive his sight.

In **Acts 9:15**, Jesus revealed to Ananias what His plans were for Paul.

In **Luke 1:30–33**, The Angel revealed to Mary the mother of Jesus the purpose and plan for Her son Jesus.

In **Luke 1:13**, The angel reveals to Zacharias that he would have a son.

In **Matthew 1:20–23**, Joseph was told about Mary's pregnancy and the call on Jesus's life before He was born in a dream.

In **Acts 27:10**, Paul perceived in his spirit that if they set sail now, even though the wind seemed mild, the voyage would bring much harm.

In **Acts 10:9–16**, the Lord revealed to Peter his plans for the Gentiles.

God revealed to several Prophets of the Old Testament the birth, death, and resurrection of Jesus Christ.

In **John 13:18–21**, Jesus knew that Judas would betray Him, and Peter would deny him three times before the cock crowed.

In **2 Kings 20:1**, King Hezekiah was given a word of wisdom to set his house in order because he was not going to live much longer.

In **Acts 21:10, 11**, The prophet Agabus told Paul what would happen to him in Jerusalem.

In **Joel 2:26** and **Acts 2:17** Joel the prophet knew God would pour out of His Spirit in the last day.

Discerning of Spirits

Discerning of Spirits is a supernatural ability given by the Holy Spirit to have insight into the realm of the spirit. When this gift is in operation, it allows one to see and hear in the spirit for the purpose of trying, judging, separating, and deciding.

This gift is specific to the spirit realm. The spiritual classifications are the human spirit, divine spirit (Jesus and angels), and satanic or demonic spirits. This is not the gift of discernment or suspicion. Let's look at some biblical examples of discerning of spirits:

Moses saw God's hinder parts.

In **Isaiah 6:1**, Isaiah said, "I saw the Lord high and lifted up."

In **2 Kings 5:26**, Elisha knew Gehazi was lying.

In **2 Kings 6:17**, Elisha said, "Open his eyes that he might see."

In **Acts 7:56**, Stephen saw Jesus sitting at the right hand of the Father.

Jesus discerns demonic activity (sickness, lunacy, unclean, deaf, and dumb).

Paul was taken up to the third heaven.

In **Revelation 1:1**, John the revelator saw things he wrote in the Book of Revelation.

Daniel spoke with an angel.

The Inspirational Gifts of the Spirit (1 Corinthians 12)

Inspirational gifts are gifts that say something: prophecy, tongues, and the interpretation of tongues. These gifts of the Spirit can be referred to as vocal gifts because they use our voice, tongue, and mouth to operate.

God wants us to know that He is revealing things, saying things, and doing things.

You may notice the three vocal gifts are not grouped together in this chapter. However, when the Apostle Paul wrote about them in the 14th chapter of Corinthians, he grouped them together. As I teach about these gifts, I will also group them together.

In 1 Corinthians 14, Paul focuses on **prophecy, prophesying, speaking in tongues, and the interpretation of tongues.**

Let us discuss the subject of prophecy by first defining what it is and isn't.

Prophecy: *To prophesy; to speak, foretelling future events. It is a supernatural utterance in **a known tongue**.*

Preaching is not the same as prophesying, although one who preaches proclaims the gospel of the Lord Jesus to win lost souls.

It is very important that we know, as the Apostle Paul teaches, there are different levels or categories of prophesying. If this fact is not established prior to reading the scriptures or teaching, it can appear that certain passages are one hundred eighty degrees opposite each other. This may cause some to believe that the bible contradicts itself.

1 Corinthians 12:29 *...do all prophesy?*

1 Corinthians 14:31 *...you may all prophesy.*

1 Corinthians 14:39 *...covet to prophecy, and forbid not to speak with tongues.*

Why would Paul tell the Church to desire something they couldn't have?

The two levels or categories of prophecies are:
1. The simple gift of prophecy
2. The prophetic gift of prophecy

The major difference is:

1. In the simple gift of prophecy, anyone can desire to flow in it. It normally has no revelational gift. As mentioned in **1 Corinthians 14:3** *But he that prophesieth speaketh unto men to **edification, and exhortation, and comfort.*** (Emphasis mine.)

2. However, the prophetic gift of prophecy normally operates with some of the revelational gifts. You will see this level of prophecy operate with those who have some level of prophetic call upon their lives.

An example of the simple gift of prophecy is found in:

Luke 1:41, 42, 45 *...and Elisabeth was filled with the Holy Ghost: (42) And she spake out with a loud voice, and said, Blessed art thou among women, and blessed is the fruit of thy womb. (45) And blessed is she that believed: for there shall be a performance of those things which were told her from the Lord.*

Let's examine what the Apostle Paul wrote in 1 Corinthians 14:

1. 1 Corinthians 14:1 Desire to prophesy
2. 1 Corinthians 14:3 You are speaking unto men for the purpose of **edification** (building up), **exhortation** (a calling near; to summon, to encourage), and **comfort** (to console or calm).
3. 1 Corinthians 14:4 You edify the church when you prophesy
4. 1 Corinthians 14:31 You may all prophesy
5. 1 Corinthians 14:39 Covet to prophesy

The Prophetic Gift of Prophecy

Note: Normally prophecy used at this level has one or more of the revelational gifts with it. Those who operate at this level will most likely have some degree of the prophetic call upon their lives. In the Old Testament, the Prophets were used to speak for God. Their utterances normally would have a Word of Knowledge and or a Word of Wisdom in them. These prophets were viewed as the messengers of

God. God Himself would put a word in their mouths and they had the responsibility to deliver that word.

As you read the Old Testament, you will see several minor and major prophets. Some were used in the revelational gifts, some in the power gifts, and others were used in both. That's why they were labeled as minor and major prophets.

In the Book of Revelation, the Apostle John was used to reveal a word of prophecy. **Revelations 1:3** states, *"Blessed is he that readeth, and they that hear the **words of this prophecy**..."*

So, we know this prophetic word was *written and spoken.*

This prophetic word comprised of the Word of Knowledge, the Word of Wisdom, and discerning of spirits. The Book of Revelation spoke of things pertaining to the past, present, and future.

Here are some of the things John wrote about in the Book of Revelation:

1. The condition of the seven churches, what they needed to do now, and what would take place if they obeyed or disobeyed.
2. He spoke of the Prophet Balaam and the prophetess Jezebel. These two people existed before his time.
3. He spoke about the war in heaven between Michael and his angels and the dragon (the devil) and his angels.
4. He also spoke extensively concerning the end times.

There are several instances where God would speak to people through other people. The prophets of old would say, *"The word of the Lord came unto me, saying."* **Jeremiah 1:4 and 2:1, Zachariah 6:9, 1 Kings 17:2, Ezekiel 28:1.**

The Lord told Abraham what he would do in the city of Sodom. **(Genesis 18, 19, and 20.)**

He spoke to Jonah concerning Nineveh and the prophet Samuel concerning the house of Eli. **(1 Samuel 3:11-14)**

Hebrews 1:1, 2 God spoke in times past to our fathers, but in these last days spoke to us by His Son.

I Received a Word from a Prophet

A Prophet once gave us a prophetic word about a church building. It happened before I had even begun to look for or be interested in another building.

He said, "I see God blessing you with a building that seats 500 people, and the building has an upstairs." A year later, we needed a building. The building we were blessed to occupy had a sign over the sanctuary doors which read, "Occupancy 500." We later found a stairway which led upstairs, just as the Prophet had spoken.

> **Matt. 10:41** *He that receiveth a prophet in the name of a prophet shall receive a prophet's reward…*

I received the word from the man of God and because of that, I received the manifestation of that word, a church building that seated five hundred people with an upstairs. Praise be to God!!!!!!!!

A Prophetic Utterance and Action in the New Testament

A prophetic action is an act or the acting out of what the Lord has told you or showed you.

When we speak of prophetic utterances, we are referring to the revelational gifts. Let's look at a prophetic utterance accompanied by a prophetic action in the Book of Acts.

Acts 11:27, 28 Agabus gave a prophetic utterance concerning a famine, and it came to pass.

Acts 21:8-13 Agabus the Prophet not only spoke of a future event but demonstrated a prophetic act. What he said and did was not for **edification, exhortation, nor comfort.** So, we know we are not reading about the simple gift of prophecy.

We get in trouble when we try to exploit the gift or operate in the office of the prophet, when the Holy Spirit just wants to use us in the simple gift of prophecy.

Chapter 22

Prophetic Insight

When I use the term "prophetic insight," most people generally think I'm referring to insight into the functionality of the prophetic. It is much deeper than that. I was listening to a prayer conference which was to last forty days straight. On the fifth night, the Spirit of the Lord began to talk to me about the prophetic. In that moment, I was actually capturing the thoughts of God. I instantly grabbed something to write on, as one thought after another began to flood my spiritual mind. I've learned when the Spirit of God speaks, I should not only be ready to listen but also ready to write down or record what is spoken. When the thoughts stopped coming, I was left with my own thoughts. Such as, *What do I do with the thoughts I just captured? Should I share this with the people on the prayer line? This is some heavy stuff, and someone may get mad or offended at this Word.* As I pondered what I had received, the Spirit of God instructed me to write what He had spoken in this book.

Many people receive downloads from heaven, but they don't understand what to do with the information they are capturing. They may have complete understanding about what they have captured. However, they may lack the wisdom to know how to handle what they received. **Proverbs 4:7 (a)** *Wisdom is the principal thing; therefore get wisdom...* With wisdom comes instructions as to when, where, what, why, who, and how.

Important Facts Concerning the Prophetic

One ministry office that seems to be magnified and to a certain point even worshipped is the office of the prophet. Allow me to explain what I am saying when I use the words, "even worshipped."

This seems to be common among some Pentecostal and Charismatic believers. The office seems to draw so much attention that everyone wants to be a Prophet or Prophetess. However, not everyone who prophesies is a prophet or prophetess. People misunderstand the prophetic umbrella that they often come under when they are amid the true prophetic. In their lack of knowledge of the prophetic umbrella, they often leave, thinking they too are prophets.

Understanding the Prophetic Umbrella

1 Samuel 10:10 *And when they came thither to the hill, behold, a company of prophets met him* (Saul)*; and the Spirit of God came upon him, and he prophesied among them.*

In 1 Samuel 19, King Saul is constantly battling with an evil spirit which caused him to become evil towards David. Due to the influence of that spirit, Saul viewed David as an enemy. For that reason, Saul wanted to kill him. David was continually on the run and often in hiding. David came to Samuel, the prophet in Ramah, and told him everything Saul had done. David's whereabouts were revealed to King Saul, and he sent messengers to take David. They came into the midst of Samuel and the company of prophets as they were prophesying. The Spirit of God came upon the messengers of Saul, and they prophesied. King Saul sent other messengers and they also prophesied as they came under the prophetic umbrella. King Saul decided that he would go get David himself. As he arrived where Samuel and the company of prophets were, the Spirit of God came on him, and he also prophesied. Verse 24 said he lay naked all that day and night. Then they said, "Is Saul among the prophets?"

Because of what Saul experienced, the question arose as to whether Saul was now a prophet. That question was quickly answered. When Saul came out from under the prophetic umbrella, he continued his quest to kill David. As you have seen from the scriptures, under the prophetic umbrella, anyone can prophesy. However, it doesn't make them a prophet or prophetess.

In some of our churches, I noticed many who may be used to utter a prophetic word then think they are called to the prophetic office. The Apostle Paul wrote a letter to the church at Corinth that addressed this issue, which I covered in Important Facts Concerning the Prophet and in Chapter 21, Two Levels or Categories of Prophecies.

Why Is the Prophetic not Embraced in Churches Today?

1 Corinthians 12:28 *And God hath set some in the church, first apostles, secondarily prophets, thirdly teachers, after that miracles, then gifts of healings, helps, governments and diversities of tongues.*

From the scriptures we can clearly see that God put prophets in the Church. However, if God wants prophets in the church, why are they not there? The quick and religious answer is that the leadership of most churches will not allow it. That brings forth another question: Why? In Paul's letter to the church in Ephesus, he states that the prophetic office is a gift to the saints. It is also to be used for the perfection of the saints so they may do the work of the ministry. The church needs the pure and genuine flow of the prophetic so it can complete the work of the ministry. Why is something that is so vital and key to the success of the New Testament Church not embraced? I'm glad you asked! It's time for those of you who walk in that office to examine yourselves. Could some of the blame lie at your own doorstep?

While I was on a prayer conference call, I heard someone say, "You cannot fully see and comprehend the portrait so long as you are in the picture." So, from a pastor who fully embraces the prophetic and is also married to an awesome woman of God who flows in the prophetic, let me upload some truths that were downloaded to me. This truth may reveal the answers as to why churches don't embrace the prophetic.

Get Rid of the Spooky

The prophetic has been seen by many church leaders as spooky and weird. Some prophets and prophetesses are dressing in a way that draws spooky attention. They dress spooky, they walk and talk spooky, then wonder why they are not received. The ultimate goal is for others to hear what God is saying, and it is not to be overshadowed by their flamboyancy. *The contents may be rejected because of the container.* Some may never taste what's inside if they can't get past what is displayed outwardly.

Your response might be, "That's not my problem. It's their loss, not mine."

The Apostle Paul understood the importance of receiving and sharing the word inside him with the people. He gave us some important keys in **1 Corinthians 9:19-22**, summarized by verse 22b: *"I am made all things to all men, that I might by all means save some."*

Just Suppose

Suppose the Lord told you go into a church that doesn't believe in speaking in tongues nor the prophetic. Yet the pastor and the congregation love Jesus. God gave you a very important word for that pastor. Out of obedience to God, you show up at that church with the word of God in your mouth. The church that you normally attend allows for prophetic words during the time of worship and as the Spirit leads. How are you going to handle this word? Are you going to flow the way you normally flow in your church? That would be considered out of order in a church that doesn't quite believe the way you do.

You say, "I will set up a meeting with the pastor in private after the church service." The meeting is set up and you say to the pastor, "I have a very important message for you from the Lord."

He is cautiously eager to hear what you say the Lord told you to tell him.

You began to utter, "Thus saith the Lord God almighty" with all sorts of religious antics. Then suddenly you begin to utter words in tongues, followed by a sentence in a language he or she understands, then followed by tongues because that's the way you normally do in your church.

The pastor is startled and calls for his or her deacons to have you removed and to never allow you to return. Now you are mad at God, but it is you who messed it up because you did not use wisdom.

Jesus, when sending his disciples out, told them in **Matthew 10:16** *Behold, I send you forth as sheep in the midst of wolves: be ye therefore wise as serpents, and harmless as doves.*

Having a prophetic call without the wisdom to properly function in that call is one of the reasons the prophetic is not allowed in many churches today. Throughout the book of Proverbs, it says to get wisdom, that wisdom is the principal thing.

What If

What if you had spoken to the pastor in your normal voice, in your normal language and told him clearly what God had told you or showed you. The word that you spoke was so accurate that the Pastor must acknowledge that only God could have revealed it to you. The use of wisdom with the prophetic will make room for the acceptance of the prophetic.

PRAYER: Father, I pray that the Spirit of God would give Prophetic Wisdom to all who are called to the prophetic office. I pray that doors will be opened for the prophetic eyes of the church to properly and orderly speak the things that have been seen in the spirit realm into this natural realm. Amen.

The New Testament Church
and the Old Testament Prophet

Another issue stands in the way of the acceptance of the prophetic in the New Testament church. This is something I call "improper prophetic functionality." Let me explain what I mean. Most prophets don't know how to function in the New Testament age of the Church. The church doesn't know how to embrace an office that preceded it. The ministry of the prophet existed long before the age of the church. In the Old Testament, prophets ministered to a king or a nation. Every one of God's kings had a prophet assigned to them. They were the spokespersons for releasing the voice of God. They were responsible for declaring what they saw and heard from God to the king and his people. For the most part, prophets lived isolated from the people. They wanted to be influenced by God only. To be the voice of God in that day was very important to the victory of God's people. That ministry was so important that God had to address false prophets coming forward with false words, by saying *"Thus said the Lord,"* when the Lord has not spoken.

Many people who flow under a prophetic mantle seem to spend more time reading and studying the prophets in the Old Testament. They watch videos and listen to the audios of prophets and prophetesses of old. They learn their mannerisms, not realizing those prophets also learned from prophets of old who learned from prophets older than that, and so on. They learned from those who have never functioned with this new entity called the church of the Lord Jesus Christ. They try to combine the old with the new, even in their prophetic utterances. They do and say things in a manner that is half and half, half the Old Testament and half the New Testament. The prophets of old spoke, "Thus said the Lord," and on occasion preformed prophetic actions.

Prophets of today may start off with a prophetic word in a known tongue and on several occasions stop and speak in tongues. It's not always the gift of tongues followed by an interpretation but a tongue of self-edification. This is what I mean by half and half: blending the old and the new. Out of the five offices the Lord Himself set up in the church, the office that existed before the church even came into existence is the one that struggles to find its place in the New Testament church. The same but opposite can be said of the nine gifts of the Spirit. Seven of the nine existed and operated in the Old Testament. The two gifts that did not exist in the Old Testament were tongues and the interpretation of tongues. These two spiritual gifts came in with the start of the New Testament church in the Book of Acts. They too have not been accepted in most churches today.

Jesus, the New Testament Prophetic Example

In **Matthew 16:13b**, Jesus asked his disciples, "Whom do men say that I the Son of man am?"

They answered by saying, "Some say that thou art John the Baptist: some, Elias; and others, Jeremias, or one of the prophets."

The consensus was that He was a prophet. However, Jesus was so different from the prophets who preceded Him. John the Baptist was considered a prophet during Jesus's time, but John had no recorded miracles or healings attributed to him. He seemed to live in isolation and did most of his preaching in the wilderness.

The ministry of Jesus was quite the opposite. He seemed to spend a lot of time among the people, healing, casting out devils, and proclaiming the gospel of the kingdom. Unlike others, Jesus was approachable.

The prophetic ministry of Jesus was also rejected by the religious leaders of His time. So long as He operated in line with their traditions, they had no issues with Him.

> **Luke 4:16-17, 21** "…*as his custom was, he went into the synagogue on the sabbath day, and stood up for to read. (17) And there was delivered unto him the book of the prophet Esaias. And when he had opened the book, he found the place where it was written… (21b) This day is this scripture fulfilled in your ears.*

The moment He released this prophetic word in the synagogue, all hell broke loose. The people were filled with wrath, and He was no longer accepted in the Church. They rose and threw Him out of their city and wanted to throw Him off a cliff. This did not cause Jesus to hide His prophetic call; to the contrary, He used his prophetic gift to usher people into the kingdom.

In John chapter 4, He engaged in a conversation with a Samarian woman with whom the Jews had no dealings. Jesus, operating in His prophetic office, gave the woman a word of knowledge. He told her she had five husbands (past) and that the man she was now with was not her husband. This word changed the woman's life to such a degree that she ran into the city and testified to men. The bible said that many believed in Jesus because of what she had told them. Many came out of the city to hear about Jesus for themselves and afterwards they believed in Him, too.

This is a great example of how a prophetic word can be used to bring lost souls into the kingdom. That one word caused the woman to become a witness for Jesus. She proclaimed, "Come see a man who told me all the things ever I did. Is this not the Christ?"

The prophetic ministry in its purest state will always bring glory to God and is a great tool to bring others into His glory. Too often it has been used to bring glory to the prophets and prophetesses. If you have been called by Jesus to operate in the prophetic office, I encourage you to study how Jesus operated, for He is our perfect example.

Chapter 23

Tongues and the Interpretation of Tongues

The gift of tongues and the interpretation of tongues are the least of the vocal gifts. In most cases, they rely on performance of each other to be complete. As the Apostle Paul wrote in **1 Corinthians 14**, "*...greater is he that prophesieth than he that speaketh with tongues, except he interpret, that the church may receive edifying.*" The conclusion is that an utterance in tongues and an interpretation of the tongues holds the same value as a prophecy, just as two nickels hold the same value as a dime.

Before we get too deep into the subject of tongues, we must address some questions. In one of my classes, I was asked two questions:
1. Did Jesus speak in tongues?
2. Why did Jesus not speak in tongues?

With Jesus as our perfect example, these are both legitimate questions. With the help of God, I will give you my best answer. For some, answering these questions **properly** will unlock many of their doors. For others, because of their church beliefs, no answer will suffice.

Some believe Jesus spoke in tongues when He was hanging on the cross.

Matthew 27:46 *And about the ninth hour Jesus cried with a loud voice, saying, Eli, Eli, la'ma sa-bach-tha'ni? that is to say, My God, my God, why hast thou forsaken me?*

Though this may sound like tongues, it is not. The writer chose to leave this in the Hebrew language in which Jesus spoke. For whatever reason, the translators also left that segment in its original Hebrew tongue. It is not uncommon for this to happen. Here are other examples of this very thing: John 1:38 Rabbi (master), John 9:7 Siloam (sent), and Acts 9:36 Tabitha (Dorcas).

Why Didn't Jesus Speak in Tongues?

The New Testament baptism (immersion) in the Holy Ghost was not part of Jesus's dispensation. Therefore, He did not participate in it Himself. He operated in the other seven gifts that had already been released and used by other believers on the earth.

In the book of Acts, tongues was the initial evidence that a person had received the baptism of the Holy Ghost. We will discuss this later.

The Three Dispensations

It is very important that we understand the three dispensations or events.

This was set in place from the beginning of creation. When the Godhead said, "Let us make mankind after Our image and likeness," the Godhead was responsible for the creation of man. Therefore, They are responsible for the redemption of man. In this redemption plan, we see the Godhead, the Trinity, individually working to bring mankind back to their original identity.

In **the first dispensation,** God the Father was involved. He was at work in the lives of the Jewish people. He made a covenant with them through Abraham. The covenant action on man's part was **circumcision**. God Himself was involved in their Old Testament redemptive process, while speaking through the prophets of the coming Messiah, Jesus, and His plan to save God's people from their sin via Jesus's death, burial, and resurrection. The Godhead plan and purpose is to always dwell amongst their people and the outpouring of his Spirit.

Isaiah 9:6 *For unto us a child is born, unto is a son is given: and the government shall be upon his shoulder: and his name shall be called Wonderful, Counsellor, The mighty God, The everlasting Father, The Prince of Peace.*

Joel 2:28, 29 *And it shall come to pass afterward, that I will pour out my spirit upon all flesh; and your sons and daughters shall prophesy, your old men shall dream dreams, your young men shall see visions: (29) And also upon the servants and upon the handmaids in those days will I pour out my spirit.*

In the **second dispensation,** John the Baptist and Jesus came on the scene and spoke of a new covenant. Both John and Jesus came with a message of repentance and **water baptism**. This was the covenant action that man was commanded to perform. Jesus Himself was circumcised on the eighth day according to Jewish law. (Luke 2:21) Jesus was also water baptized, fulfilling all righteousness. (**Matthew 3:13-15**) Jesus came to establish a new covenant while still operating under the old covenant.

When God has ordained a thing to be done, the person who is chosen to implement the act may or may not participate in it themselves. They may not perform them nor have them performed on them. An example of this is John the Baptist. Though he was ordained to implement water baptism., you never read where he himself was ever water baptized. In **Matthew 3:14**, John says to Jesus, *"I have need to be baptized of thee."*

While functioning in the second dispensation under the old covenant, Jesus spoke of the next dispensation or the next *event. Which is the time of the Spirit?* (**John 7, 14, and 16**) This was the time when the Holy Spirit would take His place on the earth, a time when people will be filled with the Spirit of the Living God. A time when people would be led by the Spirit of the Living God, the coming of the Holy Spirit and Kingdom access. He mentioned the Holy Spirit would take His place, and He also spoke about the assignment of the

Spirit of God. Here are some scripture references about the coming of the Holy Spirit:

John 7:37-39 *In the last day, that great day of the feast, Jesus stood and cried, saying, If any man thirst, let him come unto me and drink. (38) He that believeth on me, as the scripture hath said, out of his belly shall flow rivers of living water. (39) (But this spake he of the Spirit, which they that believe on him should receive: for the Holy Ghost was not yet given; because Jesus was not yet glorified.)*

John 14:16-17 *And I will pray the Father, and he shall give you **another Comforter, that he may abide with you for ever;** (17) Even the Spirit of truth; whom the world cannot receive, because it seeth him not, neither knoweth him: but ye know him; for he dwelleth with you and shall be in you. (Emphasis mine.)*

John 16:7 *Nevertheless I tell you the truth; it is expedient for you that I go away: for if I go not away; the Comforter will not come unto you; but if I depart, I will send him unto you…*

The third dispensation is the time of the Spirit, an outpouring of God's Spirit. This is the time when the presence of God indwells his people, when they are filled by and filled with Gods Spirit. A time when they are never comfortless. A time when the same Spirit Who raised Christ Jesus from the dead dwells in His believers and quickens (makes alive) their mortal bodies. A time when His people can receive, walk, and operate in their own power, not just *exousia* (delegated authority or power given by permission) but *dunimas* (inherited power residing in a thing). When Jesus the Word was on the earth, He gave or delegated authority to His apostles.

Matthew 10:1 *And when he had called unto him his twelve disciples, he gave them power (exousia) against unclean spirits, to cast them out, and to heal all manner of sickness and all manner of disease.*

Luke 10:17 *And the seventy returned again with joy, saying, Lord even the devils are subject unto us **through thy name.***

Mark 16:17 *And these signs shall follow them that believe; **In my name** shall they cast out devils… (Emphasis mine.)*

As you can see through the scriptures, the apostles were operating under the authority of Jesus's name. However, after the Holy Ghost came, believers can operate under His spiritual authority. Listen to what Jesus said:

Act 1:8 *But ye shall receive power* (dunimas), *after that the Holy Ghost is come upon you…*

Glory to God! We are living in the dispensation of the Holy Ghost! He is still here today and here to stay,

Chapter 24

Insight about Baptism in the Holy Ghost

(Jesus's Baptism)

Icannot teach about tongues without first discussing baptism in the **Holy Ghost**. Baptism in the Holy Ghost is referred to as Jesus's baptism.

> **Matthew 3:11** *I indeed baptize you with water unto repentance. but he that cometh after me is mightier than I, whose shoes I am not worthy to bear: he shall baptize you with the Holy Ghost, and with fire...*

Jesus said He would baptize with the Holy Ghost.

> **Acts 1:5** *For John truly baptized with water; but ye shall be baptized with the Holy Ghost not many days hence.*

Jesus also said He would send the Holy Ghost in **John 14:26 and 15:26.**

The release (the order of events under divine authority) of the Holy Ghost on the earth could not take place as long as Jesus was still on the scene. Jesus first had to complete the work His Father gave Him. Then the Holy Spirit could come in the fullness of the completed work. The release of the Holy Ghost must have been very important, so important that God the Father waited until the day of Pentecost to release the third event (the dispensation). At this time, people from every nation would be present to witness.

Acts 2:1-5 And when the day of Pentecost was fully come, they were all with one accord in one place. (2) And suddenly there came a sound from heaven as of a rushing mighty wind, and it filled all the house where they were sitting. (3) And there appeared unto them cloven tongues like as of fire, and it sat upon each of them. (4) And they were all filled with the Holy Ghost, and began to speak with other tongues, as the Spirit gave them utterance. (5) And there was dwelling at Jerusalem Jews, devout men, out of every nation under earth.

Tongues, the Biblical Evidence of the Baptism (In the Early Church)

There is no scriptural evidence that anyone spoke in tongues before the day of Pentecost. Speaking with tongues was one of the initial signs that someone had received baptism in the Holy Ghost. The word *baptism* means to be fully immersed. Remember when John baptized with water? The scripture said he baptized in Ae-non near Salim because there was much water there.

He was called, John the Baptist, the baptizer, the immerser. He was not called "John the Sprinkler."

Just as it is important for people to be fully immersed in water baptism, so it is when they receive baptism in the Spirit. Tongues were a result of the baptism in the Holy Spirit. In the New Testament, anytime a believer was baptized in the Holy Spirit, the utterance of tongues followed. Here are some scripture references to support this statement:

*Acts 2:4 And they were **all** filled with the Holy Ghost, and began to **speak with other tongues** as the Spirit gave them utterance.* (Emphasis mine.)

Acts 8:14-20 When the Samaritans received the infilling of the Holy Ghost, it doesn't say they spoke in tongues. However, we know that something happened that caused Simon the sorcerer to want to purchase the power. This power was the ability to lay his hand on people for them to receive the Holy Ghost. It had to be more than seeing people get born again. One cannot see a person getting born again, for that is an inward work. However, one can witness a person being filled with the Holy Ghost. Peter said, in verse 21, "*Thou hast neither part not lot in this **matter** (utterance, speech).*" (Emphasis mine.)

> **Acts 9:17** *And Ananias went his way and entered into the house; and putting his hands on him said, Brother Saul, the Lord, even Jesus, that appeared unto thee in the way as thou camest, hath sent me, that thou mightest receive thy sight, and be filled with the Holy Ghost.*

We know the Apostle Paul spoke in tongues because in his first letter to the Corinthian church he wrote that he spoke in tongues more than they did.

> **Acts 10:44-46** *While Peter yet spake these words, the Holy Ghost fell on all them which heard the word. (45) And they of the circumcision which believed were astonished, as many as came with Peter, because that on the Gentiles also was poured out the gift of the Holy Ghost. (46)* ***For we heard them speak with tongues, and magnify God.***

> **Acts 19:6** *And when Paul had laid his hands upon them, the Holy Ghost came on them; and they spake with tongues, and prophesied.*

Note: When you are born again, it is first expressed inwardly. However, when you are filled with the Holy Ghost, it is expressed outwardly.

Who Is a Candidate for the Baptism in the Holy Spirit?

Baptism in the Spirit is for all <u>believers</u>, as said by the scriptures.

John 7:39 *(But this spake he of the Spirit, which they that **believe** on him should receive...)* (Emphasis mine.)

Acts 2:39 *For the promise is unto you, and to your children, and to all that are far off, even as many as the Lord our God shall call.*

Acts 19:1, 2 *And it came to pass, that, while Apollos was at Corinth, Paul having passed through the upper coasts came to Ephesus; and finding certain **disciples**, (2) He said unto them, Have ye received the Holy Ghost since ye **believed**?* (Emphasis mine.)

John 14:17 *Even the Spirit of truth; whom the world cannot receive...*

Note: Jesus said, "The world cannot receive the Spirit of truth," however, the world can receive salvation. Through the scriptures, we have clearly seen that the baptism or infilling of the Holy Ghost is for believers. The Apostle Paul wasn't going up to nonbelievers and asking if they had received the Holy Ghost. He was talking to believers!

Salvation, Water Baptism, and the Infilling of the Spirit Are Different

I ask Christians from different denominations this question: "What does it mean to be baptized with the Holy Ghost?"

Some say, "It means you were water baptized."

Others say, "This is what happens to you when you get saved."

It is amazing that so many church people are ignorant of this experience.

In **John 3:7**, Jesus told Nicodemus, "You must be born again." Repenting of your sins and asking Jesus into your heart is what we refer to as "getting saved." The Spirit of God comes to live inside you and changes you. When this takes place, it is not immediately seen nor visible with the natural eye. Jesus, in talking about this born-again experience, likened it to the wind. Just as you cannot see the wind, you cannot see a person being born again. However, you can see the effects of the wind and of a person who has been born again. When you are born again, you start as a baby believer and grow from there.

I **Acts 19:2,** the Apostle Paul, while passing through Ephesus, talked with certain **disciples** and asked them this question:"Have you received the Holy Ghost since you believed?"

As we can see, they were **believers**. This leads us to believe that this infilling or baptism is a separate experience from the salvation experience. As we read in verse 6, Paul laid his hands on them, and the Holy Ghost came upon them, and they spoke in tongues and prophesied.

Note: When one is born again of the Spirit it is expressed first inwardly, but when one is filled with the Spirit, it is expressed first outwardly.

It is amazing that most churches will accept John's Baptism (water) while rejecting Jesus's baptism (Holy Ghost). Is this arrogance on the part of the church? Is it arrogance because they only want to except what they can control (water baptism)? Remember in **Acts 10:47,** the Jews did not want the Gentiles to be water baptized. They thought salvation was only for them. They could control water baptism when people received salvation which they couldn't see with their eyes. However, for them, proof of salvation was being filled with the Spirit. Peter, along with some of the other disciples, said, "For <u>we</u> heard them speak with tongues." **(Acts 10:46)**

A common question that comes up frequently is derived from a question that the Apostle Paul asked while trying to address the church in Corinth about the administrative offices and the gifts of the Spirit. The question he asked was meant to be rhetorical.

1 Corinthians 12:30b *Do all speak with tongues?*

(This is a very misunderstood passage, which so many people use to discourage other believers from speaking or praying in other tongues.)

If that question were to be answered, what would the answer be? Would it be yes *or* no, or would it be yes *and* no? Many people attempt to answer this question without having the proper knowledge. Others attempt to answer this question from a biased mindset. (This means they are already opposed to anyone speaking in tongues. Tongues is a biproduct of the Holy Ghost. Some may say, "I am filled with the Holy Ghost; I just don't speak in tongues. I have the Holy Ghost; I just don't want the tongues." That's like saying I want the water, but I don't want the wet.)

First, we must understand the Bible term, *diversities of tongues.* What does that mean? *This is referred to as different kinds of tongues, both known and unknown to mankind, tongues that one has never learned, the tongues of men and the tongues of angels (heavenly tongues).*

Chapter 25

Divers Kinds of Tongues

1 Corinthians 12:28 *And God hath set some in the church, first apostles, secondarily prophets, thirdly teachers, after that miracles, then gifts of healings, helps, governments, diversities* (various, different types) *of tongues.*

1 Corinthians 13:1 *Though I speak with the **tongues of men and of angels**… (Emphasis mine.)*

Although Paul's subject matter is charity, he mentions the tongues of men and of angels. The tongues of men are used and understood by men in the earth realm. The tongues of angels are those used in the heavenly realms, yet not understood by men.

1 Corinthians 14:2 *For he that speaketh in an **unknown** tongue <u>speaketh</u> **not unto men, but unto God;** for **no man understandeth** him; howbeit, in the spirit **he speaketh mysteries.** (Emphasis mine.)*

Note: In reading from this verse, there are several things we can gather:
1. There is a tongue considered to be unknown.
2. No man can understand this language.
3. When this tongue is used, man is speaking to God.
4. He is speaking from the Spirit.

5. What he is speaking is a mystery to the mind of man.
6. Speaking in this language has nothing to do with one's mind or mental faculty.

1 Corinthians 14:10 *There are, it may be, so many kinds of voices* (languages) *in the world, and none of them is without signification.*

There are approximately 7,000 different languages spoken on the earth and every one of them has meaning because they are used by man to communicate. God also used the tongues of man to speak to men. **(Acts 2:8 and 1 Corinthians 14:21)** However, the speakers had no knowledge of the language. Paul says, "There is a tongue that no man understandeth." This is used for man to pray and speak to God. There is a known tongue (known unto man) and there is an unknown tongue (unknown to man). Whether known or unknown, this is supernatural, because you have never learned these languages.

This has nothing to do with your linguistic ability. This is a supernatural utterance by the Holy Spirit in a language never learned by the speaker. It is not understood by the mind of the speaker and *for the most part* by the hearers. This is a vocal miracle!

Heavenly Written Language

Daniel 5:5, 8 *In the same hour came forth fingers of a man's hand, and wrote over against the candlestick upon the plaister of the wall of the king's palace: and the king saw the part of the hand that wrote. (8) Then came in all the king's wise men: but they could not read the writing, nor make known unto the king the interpretation thereof.*

The hand of God wrote words on the wall of King Belshazzar's palace.

The King summoned all his wise men and language experts, but no one could interpret the writing. It was written in a heavenly language which required an interpretation These words came from God, and no man could read them, nor did they know what they meant. Daniel, who God had used to interpret dreams gave him the ability to read the words and interpret His writing.

> **Daniel 5:25-28** *And this is the writing that was written, ME'-NE, ME'NE, TE'-KE, U-PHAR'-SIN. (26) This is the interpretation of the thing: ME'-NE; God hath numbered thy kingdom, and finished it. (27) TE'-KEL; Thou art weighed in the balances, and art found wanting. (28) PE'-RES; Thy kingdom is divided, and given to the Medes and Persians.*

Tongues, a Supernatural Manifestation

The first time the supernatural manifestation of tongues was released on the earth was on the day of Pentecost. One hundred twenty people were in the upper room waiting for the promise of the Holy Ghost. Those who were filled with the Holy Ghost spoke in other tongues as the Spirit gave them the utterance. The tongues they spoke were in the category of *the tongues of man* or a known tongue. This was a language they had never learned, but it was understood by the hearers. This was God speaking to man, not man speaking to God. This was mentioned in **Isaiah 28:11, 12**, *"For with stammering lips and another tongue will he speak to this people. (12) To whom he said, This is the rest wherewith ye may cause the weary to rest; and this is the refreshing: yet ye would not hear."*

This is the gift of tongues which normally requires interpretation. However, in this case, the tongues were a sign to unbelievers. **1 Corinthians 14:21, 22**, *"In the law it is written, With men of other tongues and other lips **will I speak** unto this people; and yet for all that they will not **hear me**, saith the Lord. (22) Wherefore tongues are for a sign, not for them that believe, but to them that believe not..."* (Emphasis mine.)

Did you notice that God said, "I will speak, and they will not hear Me." This is God using man's voice to speak to men in a language known by the hearers. The language was not familiar to those who were speaking. Therefore, it can be categorized as a tongue that is known to man (a known tongue). I haven't found in the New Testament where this type of tongues was ever used again, but I'm not saying it can't or hasn't happened like this since.

> **Acts 2:4-8** *And they were all filled with the Holy Ghost, and began to speak with other tongues, as the Spirit gave them the utterance.* (5) *And there was dwelling at Jerusalem Jews, devout* (pious, religious) *men, out of every nation under heaven.* (6) *Now when this was noised abroad, the multitude came together and were confounded* (confused or bewildered), *because that every man heard them* (verse 17 and 18) *speak in his own language.* (7) *And they were all amazed and marvelled, saying one to another, Behold are not all these which speak Galileans?* (8) *And how hear we every man in our own tongue, wherein we were born?*

Note: In verse 6 it says, "every man heard **them.**" In verse 7, it says, "Are not all **these** speaking Galileans?" In verse 13, it says, "Other mocking said, **These men** are full of new wine." In verse 15, it says, "For **these** are not drunken." We need to determine who the *them* and *these* were who spoke in tongues in Acts chapter 2.

Most people believe the twelve apostles were the only ones who were filled with the Holy Ghost and spoke with other tongues on the day of Pentecost.

Some believe the apostles and all who were in the upper room were filled with the Holy Ghost and spoke with other tongues.

The mockers of Acts 2:13 said, *"these men"* which would lead some to believe those who were filled with the Holy Ghost were men.

However, Peter stood up with the eleven (apostles) and said, *"These are not drunken as ye suppose..."* Notice Peter never referred to the **these** as men.

As Peter addressed the mockers, the bible declares that the other eleven stood up with him. He then mentioned the word **these**. How could he be referring to the eleven not being drunk if they were standing up with him?

If it were only the apostles and Peter, he would have said, **"We** are not drunk as ye suppose."

What Peter said in his answer to their questions was this:

Acts 2:16-18 *But this is that which was spoken by the prophet Joel; (17) And it shall come to pass in the last days, saith God, I will pour out of my Spirit upon all flesh: and your **sons** and your **daughters** shall prophesy, and your **young men** shall see visions, and your **old men** shall dream dreams: (18) And on **my servants** and on **my handmaidens** I will pour out in those days of my Spirit; and they shall prophesy.* (Emphasis mine.)

Peter mentioned sons, daughters, young men, old men, God's servants, and handmaidens, although Peter was quoting from the Prophet Joel. Why would he use those scriptures to explain what was now happening? Based on Peter's answer, I am led to believe the outpouring of God's Spirit was not just on the twelve disciples. In Acts chapter 1:15, it mentions the names of eleven apostles, the women, Mary the mother of Jesus, and his brethren. He said, the number of names together, were **about** one hundred twenty.

Notice what is said in **Acts 2:2-4**, *And suddenly there came **a sound** from heaven as of a rushing mighty wind, and it filled all the house where they were sitting.(3) And there appeared unto them cloven tongues like as of fire, and it sat upon each of them. (4) And they were all filled with the Holy Ghost, and began to speak with other tongues, as the Spirit gave them utterance.* (Emphasis mine.)

You may say the following verses say they spoke in the tongues of men. Yes, that would be correct; they spoke in languages that were known to men. However, speaking in the tongues of men did not take place until it was sounded abroad. The words "sounded abroad" means the sound of words. It wasn't until multitudes heard them that they came to the place where the sounds were uttered. Once the multitude was in a position of clearly hearing, God began to speak a message through people that He filled with the Spirit. This message from God was to a multitude, the fulfillment of the prophecy of **Isaiah 28:11** *For with stammering lips and another tongue will he speak to this people.*

> **1 Corinthians 14:21** *In the law it is written, With men of other tongues and other lips will **I speak** unto this people; and yet for all that will they not hear me, saith the Lord.* (Emphasis mine.)

Those who were filled with the Spirit immediately began to speak in tongues prior to the multitude's arrival. Now that we know there was a time before the multitude arrived, which tongues were they speaking with before the multitude came?

Paul also wrote these words by the inspiration of the Spirit, *"For he that speaketh in an unknown tongue speaketh not unto men, but unto God: for **no man** understandeth him; howbeit **in the spirit he speaketh** mysteries."* (**1 Corinthians 14:2**)

Chapter 26

The Spiritual Gift of Tongues and the Devotional Gift of Tongues

1 Corinthians 12:10 *To another the working of miracles; to another prophecy; to another discerning of spirits; to another **divers kinds of tongues**; to another the interpretation of tongues...* (Emphasis mine.)

The gift of tongues referred to in this scripture is not available to everyone. This is given to a person as the Spirit wills, as are the other eight gifts of the Spirit. Some have misunderstood what the Apostle Paul taught and corrected the church in Corinth on the proper use of tongues. Paul was addressing the church about tongues in general. Many have put all the scriptures about speaking in tongues in one basket and mixed them all together. In doing so, churches have become ignorant and confused in the subject of tongues.

Misunderstood and Misinterpreted Scriptures (In regard to tongues and prophecy)

1 Corinthians 12:30b *Do all speak with tongues?*

If it had been written, *Do all speak with the gift of tongues?* Then it would have been a yes or no question. The answer would have certainly been **no!** Not all will be used to speak with the gift of tongues.

This is like the other gifts of the Spirit. Its use in a church setting is normally followed by an interpretation, which we will discuss later.

1 Corinthians 13:8 *…whether there be tongues, they shall cease…*

Some thought Paul was saying that tongues will be done away with, so they believe and teach that tongues have ceased. It would be ridiculous for Paul to say that tongues have ceased and then dedicate the following chapter to talking about tongues. If God had taken this miraculous gift away, when did it happen?

Some say, "The proof that tongues have ceased is in **1 Corinthians 13:13**: *And now abideth faith, hope, charity, these three; but the greatest of these is charity.*"

I repeat, it would be a waste of time to say something doesn't exist anymore, **then devote an entire chapter explaining how it should be used in the church.**

In fact, Paul says the opposite in **1 Corinthians 14:5 and 39** (5) *I would that **ye all** spake with tongues* (39) *Wherefore, brethren, covet to prophesy, and **forbid not** to speak with tongues).*

1 Corinthians 13:10 *But when that which is perfect is come, then that which is in part shall be done away.*

This is another scripture that has been misunderstood, and misinterpreted. Some believe the word *perfect* is referring to the bible (God's Word). They say, "Now that we have it, these gifts have been done away with."

I have a problem with that statement. If it wasn't for the bible, we wouldn't know these gifts existed. Furthermore, I believe the word *perfect* is referring to Jesus Christ (the Word). When He comes back for His church, there will be no need for these gifts.

I once heard a minister who did not believe that tongues were for today say, "The word *perfect* could not refer to Jesus because He is not a that."

*(**1 Corinthians 13:10** …when that which is perfect is come…)*

However, I read in the scripture where John, in his description of Jesus the Word, referred to Him as that.

1 John 1:1, 2 *That which was from the beginning, which we have heard, which we have seen with our eyes, which we have looked upon, and our hands have **handled**, of the Word of life; (2) (For the life was manifested, and we have seen it, and bear witness, and shew unto you **that** eternal life, which was **with the father** and was manifested unto us…)* (Emphasis mine.)

The word *handled* means to touch and feel. Jesus used that same word when talking to doubting Thomas. (**Luke 24:39** *handle me*)

The beloved John lets us know that before Jesus came to the earth, He pre-existed with God as the **Word**.

John 1:1-4 *In the beginning was the **Word** and the Word was with God and the Word was God. (2) The same was in the beginning with God. (3)All things were made by him; and without him was not any thing made that was made. (4) In him was life; and the life was the light of men.*

1 John 5:7 *For there are three that bear record in heaven, the Father, the **Word**, and the Holy Ghost; and these three are one.*

The Word of God says, "In the mouth of two or three witnesses every word may be established." (**Matthew 18:16**)

I listed several scriptures here to support my reason for believing Jesus is the perfect One. Therefore, the gifts of the Spirit along with the fivefold ministry will remain until He returns. Because new believers are added to the church daily, the entire church will never come into a place of maturity until Jesus comes.

Ephesians 4:11, 12 *And he gave some, apostles; and some, prophets; and some, evangelists; and some, pastors and teachers;*

(12) *For the perfecting of the saints, for the work of the ministry, for the edifying of the body of Christ.*

Chapter 27

The Use of Tongues in a Church Setting

Regarding this subject, we will be exploring other supporting scriptures, as we dissect the 14th chapter of 1 Corinthians verse by verse. Knowing what Paul said, why he said it, and to whom are very important factors in understanding that chapter.

In the fourteenth chapter of Corinthians, the Apostle Paul corrects and teaches the church about the proper use of the inspirational gifts in a church setting. The inspirational gifts of the Spirit are also referred to as the vocal gifts, for they are manifested through one's voice. They also seem to be the most frequently used of the nine gifts. Therefore, they are the most frequently *misused* of the nine. Before we discuss some of the passages of chapter 14 in regard to tongues, it is important to establish there are tongues that are devotional, and some that are public.

Devotional means they are for private use between the person and God. Public means it's non private, when God uses people to speak a message in an unknown tongue. This is normally followed by the interpretation of tongues.

1 Corinthians 14:2 *For he that speaketh in an unknown tongue speaketh not unto men, but unto God: for no man understandeth him; howbeit in the spirit he speaketh mysteries.*

These important facts are mentioned in this passage of scripture:
1. There is a tongue that a person speaks that is considered unknown.
2. When this tongue is used, the person is not speaking to man.
3. When this tongue is used, the person is speaking to God.
4. No man understands him. (His words are unknown to mankind.)
5. What the person is speaking is a mystery (It is not understood by the speaker nor the hearers.) This describes devotional tongues.

1 Corinthians 14:4 *He that speaketh in an unknown tongue edifieth himself...*

1. A person speaking in this type of tongue can edify (build up) himself.
2. This is not for edifying others, but for self-edification.

Jude 1:20 *But ye, beloved, building up yourselves on your most holy faith, praying in the Holy Ghost...* (This describes devotional tongues.)

1 Corinthians 14:5 *I would that ye all spake with tongues, but rather that ye prophesied: for greater is he that prophesieth than he that speaketh with tongues, except he interpret, that the church may receive edifying.*

1. Paul said, "I would that ye **all** speak with tongues." Apparently, he is not opposed to the idea that **all** can speak with tongues.
2. He said he would "rather that ye prophesy" (*to speak by inspiration of the Spirit in a known language for the purpose of edification, exhortation, and comfort*).
3. He said, "...greater is he that prophesieth than he that speaketh with tongues, except he interpret." Whether devotional tongues or public use of tongues, it does not edify the church without the interpretation of that tongue. If someone speaks with tongues and the interpretation is given, it has the same value as a prophecy. Here is a natural example to help you understand something

spiritual. Let's say prophecy is equal to a dime. Let's say tongues are equal to a nickel and the interpretation of tongues is equal to a nickel. When you put both nickels together, they hold the same value as a dime.

4. Paul's major hope was that the church would be edified.

Devotional and Public Use

1 Corinthians 14:13 *Wherefore let him that speaketh in an unknown tongue pray that he may interpret.*

1. Because of Paul's concern for the edification of the church, whether a known or unknown tongue, Paul says, "Pray that he may interpret."
2. Paul gives the impression that the one who speaks should pray for the interpretation.

1 Corinthians 14:14 *For if I pray in an unknown tongue, my spirit prayeth, but my understanding is unfruitful.*

1. Paul says if he prayed in an unknown tongue, it was his spirit that was praying.
2. When praying in tongues, one allows his spirit to pray.
3. When our spirit prays, it has nothing to do with the mind. Our natural mind is completely ignorant as to what is being spoken.
4. Praying in tongues is praying with your spirit. Remember we are a spirit, which lives in a body, and we have a soul (our mind, will, and emotions). Most Christian prayers are from the soulish side of man. However, praying in tongues is of the spirit, which has nothing to do with what we see, hear, or feel.
5. In this verse, Paul is addressing **praying** in tongues instead of **speaking** in tongues. This describes devotional tongues.

1 Corinthians 14:15 *What is it then? I will pray with the spirit, and I will pray with the understanding also: I will sing with the spirit, and I will sing with the understanding also.*

1. When Paul says, "What then," he is saying "the conclusion or end result of all I've said is."
2. I will pray with the spirit (in tongues) and with the understanding also. This is quite different from verse 14 when he use the phrase, "If I pray." Paul indicates that praying with the spirit (in tongues) is something that he would do.
3. He also mentions he would sing with the spirit (in tongues), and he would sing with understanding (the mind) also.
4. To pray with the spirit is to pray in an unknown tongue and to pray with the understanding is to pray in a known tongue.
5. Paul seems to indicate that after praying or singing with the spirit he would follow by praying or singing with the understanding. This could possibly mean with the interpretation of what was prayed or sung.
6. Churches today seem to rely far too much on praying with their understanding first, the opposite of what Paul said he did. This describes devotional tongues.

1 Corinthians 14:16, 17 *Else when thou shalt bless* (give thanks) *with the spirit, how shall he that occupieth the room of the unlearned say Amen at thy giving of thanks, seeing he understandeth not what thou sayest? (17) For thou verily giveth thanks well, but the other is not edified.*

1. Paul seems to indicate that one can give thanks to God with one's spirit (in tongues).
2. Paul speaks of the room of the unlearned, the company of those who are ignorant of praying with the spirit.
3. He said when one gives thanks with the spirit (in tongues), they gave thanks well (excellently, rightly, honorably, or commendably).
4. Again, Paul's concern is for everyone in a church gathering to be edified (build up, encouraged).

1 Corinthians 14:18 *I thank my God, I speak with tongues more than ye all…*

1. Paul is thankful (to be grateful) to his God, that he speaks with tongues more than those in the church of Corinth.
2. If Paul spoke in tongues more than everyone in the church at Corinth, he must have spent a lot of time speaking / praying in tongues.

1 Corinthians 14:19 *Yet **in the church** I had rather speak five words with my understanding, that by my voice I might **teach** others also, than ten thousand words in an unknown tongue.* (Emphasis mine.)

1. Paul was grateful to God for the ability to speak in tongues, and apparently he used the gift frequently. Yet in a church setting where the focus is on teaching the congregation, Paul said he would prefer to speak five words in a known tongue than ten thousand words in an unknown tongue.
2. Keep in mind Paul says, "in the church" or a setting where people are there and need to be taught.
3. In some settings or gatherings, everyone there is familiar with the use of tongues or speaks in tongues themselves. The purpose of their gathering is to pray, praise, or worship, and all are edified.

Ephesians 5:18, 19 *And be not drunk with wine, wherein is excess; but be filled with the Spirit; (19) Speaking to yourselves in psalms and hymns and spiritual song, singing and making melody in your heart unto the Lord…*

Ephesians 6:18 *Praying always with all prayer and supplication in the Spirit…*

1 Corinthians 14:21, 22 *In the law it is written, With men of other tongues and other lips will I speak unto this people; and yet for all that will they not hear me, saith the Lord. (22) Wherefore* *tongues are for a sign, not to them that believe, but to them that believe not: but prophesying serveth not for them that believe not, but for them which believe.*

1. When Paul says, "In the law it is written," he is not referring to the law of Moses, but the law of the prophets.
2. The law of the prophet said God would speak using the vocals of men who were not from the area, nor did they know the language. This was recorded in Isaiah 28:11, and the event took place in Acts 2. This is the first time the Holy Ghost was released in this fashion.
3. After the infilling of the Holy Ghost, those who spoke with tongues did not know what they were saying. However, all the nations that were present at the feast of Pentecost understood what was spoken.
4. Although the words that were spoken were in an unknown tongue to the speakers, they were a known tongue to the hearers. They were not speaking to God. In fact, it was God speaking to man. This is the **public use of tongues.**
5. For all that was done and spoken, God said, ***they did not hear me.*** Apparently, there was something the Lord was saying that He wanted them to hear. (To listen, to give heed to.)
6. When Paul said, "Wherefore tongues are for a sign (a mark, a token, a miracle or wonder by which God authenticates) ... for them that believe not," he is speaking of a specific type and use of tongues. This type of tongues was used as a sign for those who did not believe. We as believers do not need a sign, for we believe in God.
7. The simple gift or the prophetic gift of prophecy is used as an aid for believers.

1 Corinthians 14:23 *If therefore the whole church be come together into one place, and **all speak** with tongues, and there **come in** those that are **unlearned** (ignorant, lacking* knowledge), *or unbelievers, will **they not say** that ye are mad.* (Emphasis mine.)

1. It seems there's not a problem with the whole church coming together in one place and all speaking with tongues. Paul's concern was when those who came in had no knowledge of the gifts.
2. Instead of receiving the knowledge of God and being taught, they will say, you are mad (Not in one's right mind, crazy, beside oneself).

1 Corinthians 14:24, 25 *But if all prophesy, and there come in one that believeth not, or one unlearned, he is convinced of all, he is judged of all: (25) And thus are the secrets of his heart made manifest; and so falling down on his face he will worship God, and **report*** (make known), *that God is in you of a truth.* (Emphasis mine.)

1. It is interesting that Paul addresses the issue with "all in one place speaking in tongues" and **those** (meaning more than one) come in that are unlearned, verses all prophesying and **one** (meaning a single individual) comes in who is unlearned or is an unbeliever. Whether it is one or more who come in while the whole church is speaking in tongues, the atmosphere will seem quite confusing to those who don't understand.
2. If all prophesy (speak by inspiration of the Spirit in their known tongue) and **one** comes in who is unlearned or and unbeliever, he is convinced (to convict, to expose, by conviction to bring to light) of all, he is judged (examined, discerned) by all.
3. This could be the simple gift of prophecy, which is for edification, exhortation, and comfort. However, I am more prone to believe it is the prophetic gift of prophecy, which has one of the revelational gifts manifested with it. The reason why I believe this lies in this segment of verse 25. "For in thus are the **secrets of his heart made manifest.**" This means that things no one knew

about this person were revealed. Because that person's heart was revealed, Paul said they will fall on their face and worship God.

4. Instead of saying "ye are mad," they will report or make known that God is truly in the church. For them to report this, supernatural revelations must come forth.

1 Corinthians 14:27, 28 *If any man speak in an unknown tongue, let it be by two, or at the most by three, and that by course; and let one interpret. (28) But if there be no interpreter, let him keep silence in the church; and let him speak to himself, and to God.*

1. This is how Paul said tongues should be handled in a church-type setting, when there is the possibility of an unlearned or unbeliever coming in.
2. Let (meaning to allow) those who speak (deliver a message) in an unknown tongue be only two or the most three. Then leave room for someone to give an interpretation.
3. If there is no one who can give the interpretation, keep silent in the church.
4. If the interpretation doesn't come forward, one may speak or pray with the Spirit by himself and to God. They may continue to speak quietly or **devotionally** but not **publicly** with tongues.
5. Paul's major concern was the proper use of the public utterance of tongues in the church. We know this because he mentions tongues and the interpretation of tongues.

Note: The person speaking with tongues (uttering a message in an unknown tongue) in a church setting must rely on the person with the gift of interpretation to come forth for the church to receive edification. If that person doesn't come forth for whatever reason, the person who spoke with tongues may seem out of order. For that reason, Paul said, if there is no interpreter (interpretation), keep silence in the church. In times past, I've had the interpretation of an utterance given in tongues and did not come forward with it. As I sat quietly, someone else came forth and gave the same interpretation I had. I did not offer the interpretation due to fear of missing it and uncertainty. This happens far too often for those who are new to how the gift of tongues and the interpretation of tongues operates.

1 Corinthians 14:39, 40 *Wherefore, brethren, covet* (desire) *to prophesy, and forbid not to speak with tongues.* (40) *Let all things be done decently and in order.*

1. Paul told us to desire to prophesy, and do not hinder anyone from speaking with tongues.
2. The overall reason for Paul addressing how the gifts are to be in operation in the church was for all things to **be done** decently (in a proper manner) and in order (fashion, succession, arrangement, or in the right order or rank). If things are not done properly, things become confusing. We know this, as Paul said in verse 33, *For God is not the author of confusion, but of peace, as in all churches of the saints.*

Chapter 28

Scriptural Reasons for Believers to Speak with Tongues (Known and Unknown)

1. Tongues are the scriptural evidence that one has received the baptism of the Holy Ghost, the baptism (immersion) of which both John the Baptist and Jesus spoke. **Matthew 3:11, Acts 1:8, 2:4, 10:46 and 19:6**
2. As the scripture says, you are speaking to God supernaturally with your spirit. **1 Corinthians 14:2**
3. As the scripture says, you magnify God. **Acts 2:11 and 10:46**
4. You edify (build up) yourself. **1 Corinthians 14:4 and Jude 1:20**
5. A person can pray with his spirit, in the spirit. **1 Corinthians 14:14**
6. A person may pray outside the natural realm or the natural mind. **1 Corinthians 14:2 and 14:14**
7. Tongues may be a sign to the unbeliever. **Acts 2:1-11 and 1 Corinthians 14:22**
8. God may speak to the people supernaturally via a known tongue or an unknown tongue. **Acts 2:1-11 and 1 Corinthians 14:21**
9. The message may be interpreted. If there is no utterance in tongues, there is no interpretation. **1 Corinthians 14:13, 27, 28**

10. The church may be edified via tongues with the interpretation flowing together, which is equivalent and has the same value as a prophecy. **1 Corinthians 14:5**
11. Tongues is where your power *(dunimas)* originates. **Luke 24:49, Acts 1:8 and 10:38 and Mark 16:17, 18**

Women Keep Silence in the Churches

As a result of Paul's desire to keep order in the church, he also addresses the issue of women speaking in the church. This has also been completely misunderstood and therefore misapplied in the church.

> **1 Corinthians 14: 34, 35** *Let your **women** keep **silence** in the churches: for it is not permitted unto them **to speak**; but they are commanded to be under obedience as also saith the law. (35) And if they will **learn** any thing, let them ask their **husbands at home**: for it is a shame for women to speak in the church.*

This passage of scripture has been used to hold many women in bondage. Based on this passage of scripture, some believe that women should not speak or teach in the church. They are to keep silent while in the church. However, it is very important to know the what, the when, the why, and the who of the scriptures. It is also important to allow the scriptures to interpret the scripture. Here are some questions that need to be answered to properly apply this scripture:

1. What was the arrangement or the setup in the church at that time?
2. What was going on in the church that would cause the Apostle Paul to make such a statement?
3. Who was Paul taking to when he said women keep silence?

As you may have noticed, I have made bold some key words in the above scripture which we need to define. As we discuss the meaning of these words, they will aid us in answering the three above questions, unfolding the truth about women preaching or teaching in the church.

Women: *virgin, female of any age, wife, or **wives***
Silence:*to hold one's peace*
Speak: *to preach, **to talk**, to utter words, to emit a sound*
Learn: *to **understand**, to increase one's knowledge*

The word *women* should have been translated as wives. We can come to that conclusion because Paul says, "ask their husbands." When Paul says, "It is not permitted for them to speak in church," he is not addressing the issue of them preaching. He is addressing talking.

If we know some of the history of the church, we will understand the issue Paul was attempting to address. First, it was common for the women to sit separate from the men, even those who were married. In some of their settings, the women would sit across the aisle from the men. In those days, the women did not understand some of the things that were being discussed. In their efforts to learn or get understanding, they would ask their husbands who were seated across the aisle. In doing so, it would become a distraction to others. Therefore, Paul said, "If they will learn anything let them ask their husbands at home; for it is not permitted for the women to talk or make noise in church."

Verse 40 holds the key to the entire chapter: "*Let all things be done decently and in order.*"

Chapter 29

Food for Thought on Languages

Paul wrote in **1 Corinthians 14:10** *There are, it may be, so many kinds of voices in the world, and none of them is without signification.*

As I mentioned earlier, there are approximately 7000 languages on the earth. Although there are so many languages used by man to communicate with each other, in the beginning, the whole earth was of one language and speech, according to **Genesis 11:1**.

As a result of early man's wrong ambitions, God confounded (confused) their language so they could no longer understand each other. Did God bring new languages to the earth? Did he bring new sounds that created new languages? The word *confound* also means to mix. Could it be that God took the original language / sound and mixed it to create new languages? In today's technological society, artists use mixing boards to create new sounds from existing sounds.

Could the heavenly tongues be the first language all of mankind spoke at the beginning of time? Could it be that God reserved the original tongue, the original sound, for himself?

I conclude, could it be that God has reserved the original tongue for Himself?

My prayer to God is that the information in this book has been a blessing to you. I pray that the eyes of your understanding have been enlightened. As you search the scriptures, I pray that the Spirit of the Living God would cause the Truth of His Word to explode on the inside of you. Most importantly, if you have never asked Jesus Christ to come into your heart and to be your savior, do that right now. Ask Him to forgive you of your sins.

Romans 10:9 *That if thou shalt confess with thy mouth the Lord Jesus, and shalt believe in thine heart that God raised him* (Jesus) *from the dead, thou shalt be saved.*

www.ingramcontent.com/pod-product-compliance
Lightning Source LLC
Chambersburg PA
CBHW060532130626
46553CB00002B/724